To Scott

Good Luck with that!

"Baseball is more than numbers and stats, it's family. Handed down from fathers and mothers to sons and daughters. When I was 12 years old my dad took me to my first night baseball game at Seals Stadium in San Francisco. I'll never forget, it glowed in the night like a beautiful emerald jewel. I'll always remember that and that's why I enjoy *Talking Baseball Amongst Friends.*"

> -Jerry Coleman
> Former Major League All-Star
> Hall of Fame Broadcaster

"What a compelling collection of short stories about baseball! Steve Sullivan has captured so many priceless, freeze-frame memories told first-person by fans, players, and the stewards of our great game. Baseball memories endure a lifetime as so vividly depicted in *Talking Baseball Amongst Friends.*"

> -Jeffery S. Moorad
> General Partner
> Arizona Diamondbacks

"I'm not sure which is the most fun, playing baseball, broadcasting baseball, or talking baseball. I'll vote for *Talking Baseball Amongst Friends.*"

> -Charlie Jones
> National Sportscaster
> Best Selling Author

"A Breezy walk along the basepaths that can be read between innings. Baseball fans everywhere will enjoy Steve Sullivan's *Talking Baseball Amongst Friends.*"

> -Dan Shaughnessy
> Author, *Reversing the Curse*

"This is an interesting read about the many stories and thoughts from players, coaches, broadcasters and people in baseball. It lets the reader see what mattered to them and what they remember most when *Talking Baseball Amongst Friends.*"

> -Fred Lynn
> Retired Professional Baseball Player
> Former MVP

Talking

Baseball

Amongst Friends

Steve Sullivan

Shamrock
Publishing Group

Shamrock Publishing Group
An Imprint of Seven Locks Press
P.O. Box 25689
Santa Ana, CA 92799
(800) 354-5348

Individual sales: This book is available through most bookstores or can be ordered directly from Seven Locks Press at the address above.

Quantity Sales: Special discounts are available on quantity purchases by corporations, associations and others. For details, contact the "Special Sales Department" at the publisher's address above.

Cover Design by Scott Weisgerber and Kira Fulks
Interior Design by Kira Shimoni Fulks
Cover Photograph by permission from George Eastman House

Printed in the United States of America

Library of Congress Cataloging-in-Publication Data is available from the publisher

ISBN: 1-931643-85-7

Dedication

For my "folks" Mom and Paul
and my wife, Angelica

Contents:

Acknowledgements

This is my first book and I certainly could not have tackled this process alone. I have been incredibly fortunate with people's willingness to contribute a story for this book and others have graciously and unselfishly lent a hand in completing this first book in the *Talking...Amongst Friends* series. If you are mentioned here, you have helped me beyond words and I will never be able to truly thank you enough.

Scott Weisgerber, John and Sheryl Young, B.R. Koenneman, Al Rosario, Mike Roberts, Ty Torres, Gary Crawford, the entire Burkle family (especially Carl, Elaine and Cally), Becky and Don Lansing, Julie Bonnart, Scott Shapiro, Michael McIrvin, Javier and Grace Rios, Paul Sterman, Patty Aubrey, Jim Riordan and Kira Fulks.

Introduction

Many people have asked what inspired me to write a book like this, and I always have to admit that I am not really sure. I have had various ideas for creative projects over the years, some crazier than others, like when a friend and I thought about starting up an aquarium cleaning business but didn't know the first thing about fish. However, this one just seemed to make complete sense from the very beginning, and perhaps more than that, like something I simply had to do.

In retrospect, I think some of the motivation for this book stemmed from trying to deal with the tragedy of September 11, 2001. Obviously, the months following that disaster were a time of great confusion and anxiety for the entire country, and indeed for many people throughout the world as they realized that even the strongest country on earth could be struck this way. In short, many people found their view of the world shaken irrevocably, and I found myself desperately needing something to cling to for normalcy, for stability. I found that something in the wonderful game of baseball. I drew great comfort in knowing that soon, ballplayers would again be running down the same ninety-foot baselines that their predecessors had traversed for over 150 years, that pitchers would soon be back on the mound launching a ball across the sixty feet, six inches to the plate at ungodly speeds, that home runs and masterfully turned double plays would be discussed over coffee or a beer just as they had been all of my life.

When the season finally did resume after a brief hiatus to honor those who died, I found myself captivated each time I heard the National Anthem before a ballgame and my heart raced during each rendition of "God Bless America" and "Take Me Out to the Ballgame." I was moved beyond words as I watched my baseball heroes embrace America's heroes, the policemen and firemen all across the country. Baseball not only honored these great men and women and renewed our sense of ourselves as a people, but it became my release when I was forced to face a world that had drastically changed.

That postseason I watched the New York Yankees become "America's Team," not for what they were doing on the field but for what the players were doing off the field to honor everyone who had fallen that terrible day in September. More than anything else, it seemed to me, it was baseball that drew us closer. It was baseball that allowed people a safe haven to release everything that they had bottled up inside of them and just cheer their hearts out for their team.

In fact, if the attacks had taken place in November when the baseball season was already over, I don't know if the nation could have recovered as quickly as we did. Now don't think that I can't appreciate how many people love football with a fervor that borders on madness, but the mass of Americans who *love* baseball do so in a fashion that seems immeasurable, that perhaps crosses the line and becomes a kind of obsession that they can't live without. Unlike football, there are baseball games each day and night during the regular season and there are always several teams battling to make it to the "second season," arguably the most exciting time in the game, because anything can happen. There are upsets in football, but only in baseball are there miracles. After the disaster of September 11, people reached out to the ballplayers and these players responded and reached right back. Baseball was once again the national pastime and record crowds came out to the many ballparks across the country to rejoice in their freedoms and their love of the game.

I have always loved baseball. When I was a little guy, probably all of four years old, I used to open our front door and walk into the main hallway of the apartment building that we lived in and "borrow" the next-door neighbor's sport section from the *Chicago Tribune*. I would take the neatly creased pieces of newsprint into the living room and flip right to the baseball section, where I would lie on my belly trying to read, yelling into the other room to ask my poor mom what various words meant, like B-U-L-L-P-E-N or H-I-T-T-I-N-G-C-L-E-A-N-U-P, or what a '6-4-3 double play' was. I was lucky enough to get an answer for some of these new terms, but a majority of the time I just heard, "Well, sound it out and then keep reading and try to figure out what it means." Basically she was telling me, "Son, I have no clue what you just said, and now is as good a time as any for you to learn what it means and let me get back to putting this pot roast in the crock pot so when I get home from work we can eat at a decent time." Luckily for me, I had a hometown super station that televised a majority of the games in the middle of the afternoon to fill in the blanks.

Baseball has affected just about every aspect of my life. In fact, I think one of the only reasons I enjoyed school as much as I did was because one of my math teachers taught me how to figure out a baseball player's batting average and a pitcher's earned run average. I remember thinking that school couldn't be that bad if teachers helped me figure out a few of the challenging terms from the *Tribune* sports page or showed me how to figure out what my baseball idols were hitting at any point in a season.

Before I started writing this book, I hadn't thought about why I love the game the way I do for a very long time. I think the last time that I really pondered the question was when I walked off my high school baseball field for the last time as a senior, knowing that I had just finished my career as a ballplayer. I am not sure I have been sadder than I was that day, but strangely, perhaps never happier either. After all, this might have been the end of my playing career, but I got to play—how many people who love this great game like I do have only been able to watch. Regardless, I have been "just a fan" of the game like many of you. We were fans through the labor disagreements, through Cal's streak, and now as Ichiro and Hideki Matsui infuse the Japanese style of baseball into America's pastime. And we will still be fans when the next great achievement appears on the horizon, beckoning us all to watch, to cheer like we have lost all sense, and again to talk about it over the dinner table or at the corner bar.

Traveling across the country and visiting different Minor League and Major League ballparks and college campuses to interview these players and baseball executives has only re-enlivened my already pretty lively passion for this game. I have had the unique opportunity to talk with fans all across this great land, and you would be surprised to hear how many guys would love to dig in at the plate and face off just once against the likes of Greg Maddux or Eric Gagne to see if they could hit off them. In fact, I find myself longing for the smell of pine tar and the heft of a bat in my hands. Even though some of us haven't played organized ball for decades, baseball is the kind of game that makes us think that, given an extended spring training, we could probably get back in the batters box and show some of these guys how to really play. But getting the chance to sit down and talk with some of the current stars in today's game was one of the most enlightening and enjoyable experiences of all. It turns out that this game we follow so closely is made up of men who still have a lot of little leaguer in them too, and when they hit one solidly and are rounding the bases, digging for the next bag, you would be pleasantly surprised to know that a lot of these guys aren't so much concerned about showing up on ESPN's *SportsCenter* as much as helping the other twenty-four guys on their team perform that most important of tasks—winning the game.

It's fantastic that baseball has again achieved great popularity in America and that increasing numbers of fans are watching and cheering and playing the game around the globe. No matter where the game is played, the bases are still ninety feet apart, the mound is still sixty feet six inches away from home plate, and the crowd still rushes to its feet in unison to celebrate great plays. There is nothing like being at a ballpark and watching your favorite player do something heroic like striking out the side to end a possible threat or hitting a long, upper-deck bomb right into the outstretched mitt of a young fan who was smart enough to bring her glove so she could go home with a wonderful souvenir.

As I put this book together, I decided that I wanted the end result to be a unique record of baseball fans, whether Major Leaguers or folks like you and me, retelling, reliving, and passing on their experiences from reader to reader. In order to enjoy this book, you do not have to be a "die-hard" baseball fan who knows what type of pitch Mark Mulder likes to throw to a right-handed hitter with two outs and a runner on first. You only need to enjoy having a conversation with someone new and "listening" to a few memorable stories that other people wish to share with you.

In, *Talking Baseball...Amongst Friends*, I am hoping you will find some touching moments, some laugh out loud funny moments, and perhaps a few intriguing insights into another person's soul. Ultimately, I want this book to be more than a simple compilation of strangers' stories. However, I want this to be like old friends sitting around a campfire at the end of a fun-filled day, telling each other stories from their lives, some about experiences they've shared and some they haven't, but all tales that the listeners can relate to because of their kinship. The kinship represented in *Talking Baseball…Amongst Friends* is perhaps born of many things humans feel and are prone to, but it is the product of one in particular —our shared love of the greatest game ever devised.

So, in the spirit of sharing interesting stories about this magnificent game, let me start the ball rolling…

While I was a student at the University of Southern California, I took the train from Union Station in Los Angeles down to Orange County where I worked a few days a week. One morning, as I looked for an open seat, I saw a man who looked extremely familiar, but I couldn't quite place him. I proceeded to sit down in the aisle seat across from him and opened up the sports section. Then it hit me as we pulled away from the station and passed just to the right of Dodger Stadium. The reason he looked so familiar was because he was Mike Scioscia, manager of the Angels and former all-star catcher for the Los Angeles Dodgers. I had watched him hundreds of times on television when I was a kid growing up in Chicago, but I had never seen him out of his big league uniform before this train trip.

He was taking the early train to Edison Field in Anaheim for the 2001 home opener, and on the way to the ballpark, we engaged in one of the most enjoyable conversations I have ever had with anyone. We touched on a variety of subjects, including baseball, business, managing people, the importance of respect and hard work, and in the midst of this discussion, one I might have with a close friend, I remember thinking what an amazing experience this was and how I didn't want the conversation to end. It blew me away that he had so much experience and knowledge and was willing to share it with a complete stranger.

When it finally came time for him to get off the train at Edison Field, we said our farewells and wished each other luck. Quite honestly, I figured that was a one-time experience that could never be duplicated or topped. Well, I figured wrong.

One of my friends, Mike Roberts, had season tickets to the Angels, and a few perks came with the season passes, such as the chance to meet some of the players and coaches at an autograph session. It just so happened that Mike needed to be out of town on business when the autograph session was scheduled, so he asked me take his 8 year-old son, Michael, to meet some of the players. Of course, I readily agreed. Aside from the fact that I would do much for my friend, especially to help out with his son, this was not so much a favor I was doing for him as a gift he was giving me.

Michael and I waited in the long winding lines for the chance to meet the players and coaches and to get a few autographs. When we finally got to the front, I watched Michael dazzle a few of the old-timers. For example, Ron Roenicke, a coach on the Angels' staff, teased Michael about the USC t-shirt he had on, which I had given him. Roenicke asked him, "What good baseball player ever went there?" And to the amazement of everyone, Michael replied, "Mark 'Big Mac' McGwire, Randy Johnson, Tom Seaver and Aaron Boone—and wait until you see Mark Prior!" My shock came from the fact that I wasn't all that convinced that he was listening to me when I had told him these little gems of information in the first place.

As the session was wrapping up and the players started to head to the locker room to get ready for that evening's ballgame, I saw Mike Scioscia coming back in to greet some additional fans and sign a couple more autographs. Michael and I headed over to say a quick "hi," and while we were walking over to meet Scioscia, I was half wondering if he would remember our conversation on the train. When our turn came to greet the Major Leaguer and to ask him for an autograph, he saw me, obviously recognized me, and smiled. He extended his hand right away and said, "Steve, right? How have you been? Still riding the train?" Ok, I won't lie to you. I was completely dumbfounded, as was the 8 year-old Michael. Before Michael's jaw could drop any lower, I introduced the two Mikes—one a manager of a Major League baseball team and the other not yet allowed to throw a curve ball to protect his young arm from injury. We talked for a little bit, and Scioscia joked around with Michael. As we walked away, Scioscia said matter-of-factly, "And Steve, if you ever need anything, let me know." I smiled, took Michael's hand and led him through the crowd and up to our seats.

At the end of the fourth inning, after polishing off a hot dog, half a bag of salted peanuts and most of my Coke, Michael looked up at me with his big ol' brown eyes and said with youthful wonderment, "Uncle Steve, Mike Scioscia just said to you that if you ever need anything to let him know. How cool is that?!" I put my arm around him, gave him a hug, and we looked back out onto the field and just laughed. We still laugh about that moment to this very day.

So, using this first story as our point of departure so to speak, I would like to take you on a journey and share some different baseball moments that have made my life a little brighter and which I hope will give you some pleasure too — my stories and those told by other fans of the game as well as stories that ballplayers and others associated with the game have to tell. As Ken Smith put it in his 1956 book, *Baseball's Hall of Fame:* "The first game of baseball was played on old man (Elihu) Phinney's farm but if, in his Almanac some garbled type had come out to read that on his cow pasture (now Doubleday Field) thousands of people would some day gather to see a group of boys romp with a ball, while a million others as far West as California would sit in their parlors and follow every play out of the very air, why the issue would have been scrapped as the most nonsensical balderdash ever to find its way into type." If you are reading this, welcome to the crowd of nonsensical balderdash-loving fans. Like I alluded to earlier, this book is a like an outing where friends share their stories, so I invite you to pull up a chair and come join this talk around the campfire —because we're just getting started here. We're talking baseball... amongst friends.

Chapter One

When Only the Ball was White

Hank Presswood
[Former Negro League Player]

Henry "Hank" Presswood initially played for the Mill City Jitterbugs and Denkman All-Stars. After proudly serving his country as a member of the United States Army, he joined the Cleveland Buckeyes, and he finished his career with the famed Kansas City Monarchs. After spending quite some time with Hank Presswood, one of the things that stands out most is the smile that comes across his face whenever he talks about baseball.

There were so many great ballplayers back then in the Negro Leagues. The things these guys could do was something to see. 'Big Josh' (Josh Gibson) could hit any pitch. As far as I am concerned, he is the best I ever did see. He hit a ball further than I have ever seen a ball hit. It was such a shame that a lot of these guys didn't get a chance to play Major League baseball. They were so good and there were *SO* many of them that could have played. I remember being down in Birmingham, Alabama teasing Willie (Mays) about that bucket catch of his. He went on to be one of the greatest ballplayers that ever played. Willie was another one of those players that was just something else.

I'll never forget when I went over to Kansas City last year to the museum (Negro League Baseball Museum), and I saw my glove and my old ball shoes there behind the glass. That is something, really something. Those years that I spent in the league were exciting for me, that's for sure! I still remember my first game in the league. I was playing shortstop, and I was so excited. When the first ball was hit towards me, I came charging in, and when I finally stopped bootin' the ball, the man was on second base. I looked up and saw that big crowd. I had never played in front of that many people before. After that I settled down and there was nothing to it.

Another one of the great players in the league was Satchel Paige. Boy, could he throw. I just wanted to get a base hit off him. I didn't care who he was when I was up to bat, but believe me, I was sure excited to see him at the ballpark. I remember there was one time we (the Cleveland Buckeyes) were on our way to Kansas City to play Satch and the Monarchs. Even our big boys who were hitting .300 were quiet during the trip, but not me. I was the only one on the bus talking. When we got there, the Monarchs were already out on the field warming up. We pulled up and the team started to get off the bus, and when I walked off the bus, I remember hearing this sound: *Boom...Boom...Boom.* I went up to our manager and said, "Hey, skipper, it is not July the fourth, so why are they shooting off fireworks inside the ballpark?" He just chuckled and said, "They ain't shooting off fireworks in there. That's ol' Satch warming up." All of our big men kept walking off the bus, shaking their head after they heard that. We finished bringing in our equipment then, and we were sitting in the dugout watching Satch warm up. It was so quiet you could hear a rat crawling on cotton.

When Satch got done warming up, he reached down and grabbed his jacket. He put his jacket on and started to walk over where we were all sitting down just watching him. He came through our dugout, walked down to one end and turned around and walked back to where he came in. When he had walked back the second time, he reached in his back pocket and said, "Boys, I got that ball today." I said to him, "Oh yeah?" He looked back at me and said, "Hank, I remember you. Don't think about hitting one of those low line drives and runnin' like a deer. Not today!"

At this point, I stood up and walked towards him and said, "You know what, Satch? When it is my turn to hit, I am going to go up to that bat rack...," and I turned and pointed at this old wooden bat rack that was just ready to fall apart, "and I am going to get me a 34-inch bat, and boy I am going to give you a whooping you never had before." I believed I could do it. I knew I was gonna get my hit.

After the first inning, the first three hitters went down like it was nothing. Satch made it look easy. The first three Monarchs all sat down too. In the second inning, after the first two guys couldn't hit Satch, it was my turn to hit against him. I did just like I said. I went over to the bat rack, grabbed a 34-inch bat, and I came up to the plate and looked right at him. He just looked back at me and said, "Ooooh no. Not today." I said back to him, 'The only way I don't whoop you today is if you keep that ball in your back pocket! You ain't gonna throw it by me."

He reared up and threw one right at my head, just trying to frighten me, but you know what? I wasn't afraid. All I wanted, all anyone wanted, was to get a hit off of him. I had heard so much about him before I got into the league. I always wanted to get a base hit off old Satch. He reared up again and fired one again right down the middle of plate. All I could do was shrink in my shoulders. I said to myself, "Good God almighty…"He looked down on me from that hill and just laughed. So I hollered out to him, "I am still going to whoop you." He said back with a grin, "Not today, Hank."

On the next pitch, he threw me a curve ball and I hit a line foul. I swung so hard I had to tug on my pants again to make sure they were still up. I reached down and grabbed some dirt and rubbed it into my hands. I dug in. You didn't dig in against Satch. He reared up again, and he threw one so hard I tell you all I could do was shrink in my shoulders again as it hummed just past my head. I still had two strikes on me, and I remember thinking to myself, 'Here it comes. I'm ready.'

He knew he had two strikes on me and was just setting me up. Satch reared on up again, rocked back and started at me. He had this hesitation pitch, and after he let it go, I swear that thing floated all over the place. I didn't come anywhere near that ball. I swung so hard that I pulled a muscle in my back and couldn't pick up a bat for three days! He was out there laughing. I never did get a base hit off him. We used to say he was the only guy that could turn a baseball into an aspirin tablet. He was the greatest I have ever seen. He wasn't afraid either when he went into the Major Leagues with all of those .300 hitters up there. They even outlawed his hesitation pitch and made it illegal because he made all those great hitters look like fools.

Just take the ball and throw it where you want to.
Throw strikes. Home plate don't move.
-Satchel Paige

Johnny Washington
[Former Negro League Player]

J ohnny was a gifted athlete who pitched, played first base and outfield for the Houston Eagles and Chicago American Giants in the Negro Leagues. After his playing career ended, Johnny joined the U.S. Marines in 1951, serving in the Korean War. While in the Marines, he was wounded twice and received two Purple Hearts and a Silver Star. Despite his injuries, after leaving the military, Johnny played baseball in the Minor Leagues until 1959. Becoming dear friends with this American hero has been such an honor and pleasure. We have been able to spend countless hours together talking about the game we love.

It was about a ninety-degree summer day game down south where it feels hotter than what the thermostat reads because of the humidity. I was picked to pitch this particular day against my idol, Satchel Paige. I made my way down the right field line towards the bullpen, and after a couple of warm up pitches, I started putting a little steam behind the ball. It was real hot, and I was so excited that I was able to get loose pretty quick. You could hear the ball pop in the catcher's glove all over the park. The guy catching for me, Odell Bailey, had a glove that really sounded off. Of course, I loved to hear that sound. I loved baseball, period. I could have played a double-header every day. As I continued to loosen up, I kept throwing harder and harder. The sound of Bailey's glove just got louder and louder. Before I knew it, the entire area alongside of the bullpen was jam-packed. The kids were all excited and were hollering, and adults were oohing and aahing. I really gave them a show.

I remember looking over across to the opposite side of the field as Satchel Paige made his way to the other bullpen to start his warm up for the game. I continued to burn up Bailey's glove.

I ended up warming up for over a half an hour. I was throwing everything perfectly. Bailey would squat down and set up for a curve ball, and I swear that thing started off at the top of his catcher's mask, crossed the plate and dropped to the ground like it fell off a table. People were shaking their heads like, who is this guy? I was thinking to myself, 'If I am this good in a game, I might never lose.' I looked over at Satchel Paige, and every ten pitches or so, he'd let one loose and fire a fastball. But he was throwing all this slow stuff otherwise.

I was getting awful tired, so I decided now was the time to go over, introduce myself, and get his autograph. I walked across the outfield and made my way to the bullpen where he was still loosening up. He stopped what he was doing and looked at me. I don't know why, but I just stopped. I was about forty feet from him, and I just froze. I kind of smiled, and he said with a snarl, "You wanna talk to me?" I said, "Uh, yes, sir."

He looked at me for another second and grinned. "How are you going to talk to me from way out there? Come on over." I let out this big breath and walked over to the great Satchel Paige. He started asking me a bunch of questions about where I was from, what I liked about baseball, and then he asked me, "How many innings you intend to pitch today?" I pushed my shoulders back, took a deep breath, and said, "Nine sir." He started laughing and threw his arm around my shoulder, and once he stopped laughing, he said, "Well you just pitched five or six of 'em right now and we are going to beat the tar outta you after the fourth inning! You just left all your best stuff in the bullpen showboating for those people and ain't none of 'em brought a bat to face you."

Then he gave me some advice that I used for the rest of my career: Don't throw so many pitches when you warm up. Throw about 25 or 30 pitches, focus on location, mix up your curve ball and fastball. I thanked him, shook his hand, and made my way to our dugout. The whole way I was thinking about what he had told me, but there was no way I was going to let him be right about the fourth inning. The first three innings were easy. My fastball was moving and really running in on the hitters. I was throwing in the mid-90's without a problem. My curve ball was jumping all over the place, but I started to notice a difference in the third inning. By the fourth inning, my fastball was straight and my curveball was straighter. I was exhausted. The first three innings, they couldn't get a hit off me to save their life, but in the bottom of the fourth, they hit everything I threw up there. Luckily, they hit the ball near three people for outs to get me out of the inning alive after only two runs. The next inning, Kansas City scored two more runs and my manager came out to the mound to take me out and bring in a new pitcher. He said to me, "So, what did you and Satchel talk about?"

At that point, I realized how right my idol was when he said I would get shelled in the fourth inning, and I said, 'Man, that Satchel is something. He knew I was gonna get beat up and that I left the best game of my life back in the bullpen.' I gave him the ball and started to walk to my dugout. I looked over at Satch and he just winked at me and smiled.

After that game, whenever we played against Satchel, I would meet up with him and a group of other players after the game, and since we didn't have any money, we would sit around drinking a few beers and listen to Satchel tell stories about "Cool Papa" Bell and his old teammate "Double Duty" (Ted Radcliff). He could tell the best stories. That was one of the things I loved most, sitting around talking baseball. I guess you could say, "talking baseball... amongst friends."

Cool Papa Bell was so fast he could get out of bed,
turn out the lights across the room
and be back in bed under the covers
before the lights went out.

-Josh Gibson

Charles Johnson
[Former Negro League Player]

Charles Johnson was born on August 7, 1909. He moved to Chicago in 1925, when he was a promising young outfielder and pitcher. Johnson made several barnstorming tours in Canada and throughout the USA to continue to play baseball. At the time of this book's printing, at 97 years of age, Johnson is the elder statesman of Negro League baseball and one of the oldest living members to have played in the league.

When people ask me why I joined the Negro Leagues, I always tell them it's simple really — I was hungry. The depression was a tough time for everyone, and I was completely without funds. I had a job at National Box Company and made 25 cents an hour. At two dollars a day, that ain't much of a living, but because everything was closing down, I was let go. Luckily for me, I just happened to live down the street from the Radcliff's (Ted "Double Duty" Radcliff's house). "Duty" had two other brothers that played baseball, and they let me join their team, and we barnstormed across North America to play baseball in the United States and Canada anywhere we could. Once in a while, when the other pitchers had sore arms, they would have me come in and pitch for a bit. In 1930, we headed up to Canada and played up there against some really good teams. Even though we only made about a dollar and half a day, it sure was fun playing baseball with those guys. When we finished that barnstorming tour, I went back to Chicago and got ready to join another team to do it all over again. Back in the 30's, there were quite a few Negro teams, so I joined a team whenever I could.

There was one time I joined the Hartford Giants. They were already scheduled to drive up to Jefferson, Wisconsin to play a double-header the next day. Six of us jumped into one car and nine got in the other at about one o'clock in the morning and drove up to Jefferson, which was about 120 miles north of Chicago. Back then, the cars didn't go much over 35 miles per hour, so when we finally got off of the highway and onto their main street, we found the first spot, parked, leaned back in our seats and went to sleep. When we woke up, we realized we fell asleep right in front of the bank and there was a guy sitting in the doorway holding a shotgun just looking at us. We got out of there as fast as those cars could go. Afterwards we laughed pretty hard, because we were the only black guys in town and we were sleeping right in front of their bank.

It wasn't always funny though. There were some rather tough times. When I was playing for the All-Nation Clowns in 1933, I was one of two blacks on the team — me and Albert Moorehead. He was the catcher and I was a pitcher and played outfield when I wasn't pitching. We took a team bus to Baraboo, Wisconsin after playing a double-header against Portage (WI), and when we got to the hotel and walked to the front desk, the clerk, after taking a long look at Albert and me, told us that he didn't have a reservation for us because there were two black men on the team. We stood around and waited for the manager of the hotel, and when he finally got there, he took us outside just in front of the little hotel and told us the same thing the clerk had said earlier. He said he was sorry, but we couldn't stay at their hotel because Albert and I were black. A white fellow and his five or six year-old son were standing there watching this whole thing take place. He walked over to our manager and said, "Well I heard what that so-and-so told ya'll. I am an engineer on the railroad, and tomorrow I am going to be off of work. I really would like to see a ballgame. If you all agree, I would like to take the whole team home with me for dinner and you can stay with me." He called his wife and told her to call her girlfriend over to help her cook — there was going to be a lot of us for dinner. Back in those days, we figured out right away that when a white man was traveling, wherever he stopped he was at home. A black man had to try to find a place to stay. I ended up pitching the next day for us in the first game and we found a way to win.

Charles Johnson retired as a member of the Chicago American Giants in 1944, three years before Jackie Robinson played in his first game with the Brooklyn Dodgers.

Chapter 2

From Home to Home Plate

A Mom that Loves Her Twins

Many times while growing up in the great state of Minnesota, I would come home from school in the afternoon to find my mother busy preparing dinner with the Twins game on the radio and her score card close by. She would rush to the table to make certain that she recorded exactly what had happened after every at bat, so when my dad came home from his second or third job or I came home from school, she could give us a detailed play-by-play recap! God forbid the mighty Twins have a game on television because dinner might just be a bit late, and if it was really a close game, dinner could very well end up burnt beyond recognition. My mother so loved the Minnesota Twins and the game of baseball that nothing could interrupt her concentration on a game.

Those were the wonderful summers of Harmon Killebrew, Bobby Allison, Camilo Pascual, which then turned into the days of Kirby Puckett and Kent Hrbek. The players seemed larger than life even then. These were the men who challenged the likes of Paul Bunyon and his trusty blue ox, Babe, as far as legends and stories go. This was a time when movement between teams via free agency was virtually nonexistent, and once a player came up with a particular organization, he stayed there for his entire career. Consequently, in Minnesota we grew up with certain players and cheered their every move.

One day when I was in high school and finally able to drive, I proudly announced that I was going to take my mom and my little brother Dale to Minneapolis to see her "adopted" boys play at the Hubert H. Humphrey Metrodome! She was so excited that I think sleep was a little difficult for her until that wonderful day finally arrived. It was a spectacular, clear, warm, July afternoon — a perfect day for baseball! Even though it was a three-hour drive, we left Duluth, Minnesota five or six hours before game time because none of us had ever ventured so far, let alone *without* Dad, who had to work.

We went inside as soon as we were allowed, watched each team take batting practice, and I swear the smile never left my mother's face! The script could not have been written any better either. We were surrounded by people every bit as much in love with "our boys" as my mom. The Twins beat Detroit 9 to 4, and she had the time of her life, sharing her opinion with anyone who would listen. The day ended with a long drive home, and the conversation never left the topic of my mom's Minnesota Twins.

My mom has been gone for several years now, but I have carried on her love of the Twins and miss very few games myself, thinking of her often as the balls and strikes are called, as the hits go over the fence or stay in the infield, as the game ends and people cheer. Being able to take in a ballgame is a wonderful reminder of listening to the games with my mom while I was growing up.

{Contributed by Charlie Moe}

The Olympic Spirit

In summer of 1992, I had just begun doing some work with USA Baseball. They were in process of getting the Olympic team ready for competition in Barcelona later that summer, and I was invited to their training facility in Millington, TN (in the Memphis area) to see an exhibition game or two and to meet and visit with some of the players. I drove down to Memphis, taking along my two oldest sons: Chris, then age fifteen, and Kevin, then twelve. On this particular night, Team USA was hosting Cuba.

The US team had only recently gone through the final selection process, and one very surprising note was that they had released an All-American second baseman from Pepperdine and kept some freshman from Georgia Tech instead. After arriving at the ballpark, we were given a quick tour and then I was invited into the clubhouse to meet the coaches and the players. The one player that I remember most vividly was this skinny, skinny kid from Georgia Tech who looked like he was about twelve and seemed painfully shy, but who also smiled easily and was incredibly polite. His answer to everything was "Yes sir" or "No sir." He was very respectful and very polite—just a delightful young man.

It was pretty obvious why they had kept this kid on the club once the ballgame began. What a ballplayer! He was totally at ease in the field, making difficult plays look routine. He covered a lot of ground, and he had sure hands and textbook footwork. And he was aggressive at the plate. He didn't appear to be over-matched against a much older, much more experienced Cuban pitcher

19

or a Cuban ball club featuring half a dozen Major League-quality players.

Anyway, that was the backdrop. The real story was the absolute, pure enjoyment that I had spending the time with my two sons, both in the car and at the ballpark. Since I had been traveling so much, this was just a great opportunity to catch up with them both. They, of course, were absorbed in their own lives and doing their own activities when at home, so this really was quality time. In fact, looking back on it, this was truly 'precious' time. It all goes so quickly.

Nothing dramatic happened, Cuba won the ballgame 3 to 1. The US team, composed totally of college kids, was overmatched but competed hard, and a number of those kids made it to the big leagues: Phil Nevin, Jeffrey Hammonds, Charles Johnson, Jason Varitek, Darren Dreifort, Jason Giambi — and that skinny freshman from Georgia Tech.

But the real fun, the real enjoyment, was the opportunity to spend the time with Chris and Kevin. This trip and that ballgame gave us that time together. I don't know if those two even remember the trip, although I suspect that they do, but I know that I'll never forget it.

Oh, yeah. The skinny freshman from Georgia Tech? Nomar Garciaparra.

{Contributed by Mike Berger}

Omar Vizquel
[Major League Player]

Vizquel remains the top fielding shortstop in Major League history. At the end of the 2005 season, his first in the National League with the San Francisco Giants, he still holds onto the highest fielding percentage (.987) in Major League history among shortstops who have played at least 1000 games at the position. The ten-time Rawlings Gold Glover is arguably the greatest shortstop in the history of the game with his acrobatic plays, timely hitting and unsurpassed enthusiasm for the game of baseball.

It would be hard to mention just one moment, but obviously the most memorable experience for me is my first day in the big leagues — April 3, 1988. I was playing against the Oakland A's, and that experience brought back a lot of memories of how hard it is to make it to the big leagues and how hard I had to work to get there. It was a great accomplishment for myself and right now I am in my 17th year of my Major League career and I can't ask for anything better than what I have been doing.

During the course of my career there have been other memories too…like hitting a grand slam to win the game, playing with the Ken Griffey Sr. and Jr combination and watch them hit back to back homeruns. Being in the World Series a couple of times and having one of my best plays ever in Game 6 of the World Series against the Marlins and being a part of a no-hitter. Everyday is a new experience for a Major League ball player and I love this game. I am just still proud that I am able to still play this game as long as I have.

Omar, Brad and a Dad

In 1997, seven year-old Brad Hantler played in the "house" league of the NFWB Baseball Program in the cities of Farmington Hills and West Bloomfield, Michigan. Brad played on the Indians (as in Cleveland) team of seven and eight year-old boys. He enjoyed a decent season at the plate and in the field, although one must bear in mind that few balls are actually caught by players in this age group. Brad was one of four players selected by his peers to represent the Indians in the league all-star game.

At season's end, the NFWB Program fielded tournament teams for the younger age groups to represent the cities of Farmington Hills and West Bloomfield in tournaments throughout Southeastern Michigan. Brad wanted to try out for the eight-and-under team. His parents, who had more than enough baseball in the spring and early summer, were not all that excited about the prospect of giving up eight weekends in June and July to travel to out-of-town baseball games. Continuing the season as a tournament player was important to Brad, however, but not because of his love of baseball, but because his best friend Todd was trying out for the team. You see, Brad was not all that passionate about baseball, which was a distant second or third to his real passion – basketball.

Brad, however, did try out for the team because his parents didn't want to deny him the opportunity to play for an elite team, and frankly, because they figured that, with 24 boys trying out for one team of 12 players, it was unlikely that a seven-year-old would make an eight-and-under team. To everyone's surprise, however, the NFWB Program decided to field two teams that summer, and all 24 boys would play on one of the teams. Brad was the 23rd or 24th player selected in the player draft.

Brad was a substitute outfielder on this particular tournament team. They had an outstanding summer of travel baseball, winning six of the eight tournaments in which they played throughout Southeastern Michigan. While Brad played only sparingly on the team because he was twelfth on the depth chart on a twelve-player team, he enjoyed the experience of playing on an elite team and the camaraderie of the other eleven players. His parents were pleasantly surprised by how much they too enjoyed the tournament baseball experience.

After the tournament season ended and Brad began to think about football and basketball, one of his dad's friends, Al Rosario, came to town from California. Al was in town for business and to take in a Detroit Tigers baseball game at Tiger Stadium. Al asked Brad's dad to join him at the game, and to bring Brad and his older brother, Scott. Al had a surprise in store for Brad and Scott that he shared with their dad.

Al and the three Hantlers arrived at Tiger Stadium at 4:30 p.m. for a 7:30 game. Brad and Scott wondered what they would do for three hours until the game started. They soon found out. When they entered the stadium, Al and the Hantlers descended the steps to the area of the box seats, but they did not stop there. Al opened a gate to the field as Brad's and Scott's eyes showed their wonderment.

Al took the boys and their dad onto the Tiger Stadium field while the Tigers were stretching and doing their pregame activities on the left side of the field. Al gave the boys a ball and told them to play catch. It was very exciting for Brad and Scott to be playing catch on the field of a Major League stadium, especially with the Detroit Tigers warming up just on the other side of the field.

Al soon disappeared into the Indians dugout, and the Hantlers began to wonder if this was some practical joke that would lead to their arrest for trespassing. After a few minutes of wondering about their impending arrests, Al walked out of the dugout with someone dressed in a Cleveland Indians uniform. As they approached the boys, Omar Vizquel smiled broadly and welcomed the boys and their dad.

Omar then picked up a bat, and despite the "No Pepper" signs adorning the Stadium, asked the boys to play a game of pepper with him. Unfortunately, Brad did not catch too many of the balls hit back at him by Omar. The game lasted for about 30 minutes, and Brad worked up quite a sweat chasing the balls hit to and past him. The good news is that the Tiger players on the other side of the field were not laughing.

After this daunting experience, Omar asked the boys to do some stretches with him. For the next ten minutes or so, Omar told them about his life growing up in Venezuela, how his first glove was a paper bag and his first baseball was handmade of cardboard, paper and rubber bands. He talked about his love for the game of baseball and the dedication required to succeed, and not just in baseball but in life. He also gave Brad some much needed pointers on fielding.

Omar also had a lesson for Brad's dad. Omar told him, "My dad took me out to the ball field to practice almost every day when I was a boy, and this is what you need to do with your boys. It takes more than them wanting to get better — you have to be with them while they are doing it."

Over the next six years, a fire grew within Brad, as he and his dad, and sometimes Scott, practiced almost every day that Brad did not have a game or a team practice. In the winter, they worked on fielding techniques in their basement, and they also did some batting practice at indoor cages.

The practice and dedication that Omar spoke about paid off. Brad graduated from the younger age tournament teams to the NFWB Cobras Travel Teams, playing in Michigan and in Florida in the Walt Disney World–World Series at age eleven and at Cooperstown Dreams Park at age twelve. Brad was no longer a substitute. He became the Cobras starting shortstop and batted between .400 and .500 every year. At age twelve, he hit for an astounding .641 average during the season and .500 during the Cooperstown Dreams Park World Series. He again hit above .400 at age thirteen and added base stealing to his repertoire. Brad stole home, yes, home, five out of eight attempts last year.

As good a hitter as he is, he is a better fielder, with great range and an arm to match, especially from the hole between shortstop and third base. It is not by accident that he began playing shortstop. Omar Vizquel made a difference in the life of a seven year-old boy (and his father).

By the way, baseball is now Brad's passion.

{Contributed by Steve Hantler}

Neighborhood World Series

For me as a fan, the game of baseball has gone through a metamorphosis. I started as a young kid idolizing some of the greatest players of the game—especially from my favorite team, the Minnesota Twins—and spending entire summers rounding up the whole neighborhood to play ball, all day, everyday. I was the kid who, like many of you did, tried to act out the game-winning homerun of a Harmon Killebrew or stealing a base like Tony Oliva. Today, I have the pleasure and pure joy of teaching my son about the game.

My father was not a sports fan. However, we spent many quality hours playing catch in the backyard. It never seemed like we were doing anything special—it was just easy to do. Today, I realize how special it was and what those precious minutes meant to my father, and now I have the opportunity to share that same quality time with my children.

I have always loved the feel of the mitt on my hand, the swing and crack of the wooden bat, and the satisfaction of completing a play on either side of the plate. But I can not describe the overwhelming joy and pride of watching my son make a great catch or a simple throw to first. I still remember my son's first T-ball game and almost every game he has played since.

The magic of the big ballpark hasn't changed for me either. I love making it to a game, and I still watch every play with as much enthusiasm as I did as a kid. However, now I am more aware of the kids in the stands, including my own, and I love listening to the chatter as they watch their favorite players and mine. I could go on like this forever, but one thing is clear: baseball is a very special game...

{side note}

After I wrote this and sent it to you last night, I felt especially inspired to play catch with my son. So after dinner, we were out on the front lawn throwing to each other when a few of my son's friends came by and joined in. It was such a nice summer evening that some of my son's friends' parents were out walking, and the next thing I knew, they joined in the fun with their kids. Before I knew it, we were all in the backyard under the lights finishing up a "neighborhood world series" — north side of the block verses the south side.

No one really knew the actual score. As you can imagine, it wasn't really about the score. Both teams claimed they won and all of the dads walked away tired and smiling and half-wondered if their kids really outplayed them. Of course, we all knew deep down that they had. However, as dads, we will be hesitant to admit this. The experience was a feeling of pure elation, even just listening to the conversations between the families as they walked down the driveway. The conversations certainly didn't stop until the kids were finally tucked into their beds and fell asleep on their pillows. A few phone calls came through later, and it sounds like the dads want a "rematch" game over Labor Day! Who knows, we might have a new tradition in our neighborhood that started with the help of our national pastime.

{Contributed by Steve Johnson}

Dave Roberts
[Major League Player]

oberts played his college ball at the University of California at Los Angeles and is one of seventeen current Major Leaguers who have earned a college degree. Roberts earned All-Pac 10 honors his sophomore year and again in his senior campaign while leading his team with a .353 batting average. He is the all-time stolen base leader for UCLA with 109 swipes.

I have had a ton of memorable moments in my baseball career, and it all started back in little league and when I was a kid starting out playing T-ball, when we used to all sleep in our uniforms the night before the game. We played those games on Saturday, and I had my uniform on Friday night when I went to sleep. But my most memorable moment has to be my first game in the majors. I was with the Cleveland Indians and got the call up the same night that we played the Tampa Bay Devil Rays and Wade Boggs collected his 3,000th hit. Just to be on the same field with a Hall-of-Famer like Wade Boggs and to share that date with him with my first day in the Majors is a wonderful memory. I think John Flaherty was catching that game, and my next at bat after I got my first big league hit he said to me, "Ok, you have 2,999 to go!"

Did I Hit It?

The summer after the third grade, I was a huge baseball fan and constantly trying to show off my new found talent—hitting a baseball. On one occasion, my sister and I were playing out in the front yard with a couple neighborhood friends. She was pitching to me, and I was hitting the ball across the street where our friends were shagging flies and throwing them back in for more pop ups. I must say I had quite a swing and was very eager to show off. My sister and our friends knew this and challenged me to try to hit the basketball across the street. Of course I could hit the bigger ball that far and set out to prove it!

I ran into the garage, found the basketball and tossed it to my sister. She pitched it to me, and I swung as hard as I possibly could, propelling the ball across the street, but the impact of the bat hitting the basketball caused a massive ricochet, which drove the bat back and into my face, completely knocking me out. I woke up to the vision of my terrified sister's face as she stood over me trembling. She took me inside to clean me up and to tend to my wound. I only ended up with a few butterfly bandages to close the gash, but I was eternally humbled by my experience and taught a valuable lesson in physics that day!

{Contributed by Mike Mulcahy}

Anytime you think you have the game conquered,
the game will turn around
and punch you right in the nose.

-Mike Schmidt

Philadelphia Phillies Hall of Fame Third Baseman (1972-88)

Mike Schmidt's Tribute Night Speech
[May 26, 1990]

Ihave a short message for you tonight. It concerns those areas of my life that were most important to my success. I'd like to talk about my faith, my family, my friendships and about you, my fans. Each of us has our own definition of faith. I define my faith three ways.

First, my faith in God. God is the source for all my strength –physical and mental. In 1977, God entered my life. My faith in Him provided a foundation for my life and career.

Second, my faith in myself, my confidence, my belief that I would always reach my goals if I worked hard enough, especially during the tough times.

My third faith involves those around me, my family, my teammates, and yes, YOU, my fans.

The affect of my family on my career began with Mom and Dad and my sister Sally, back in Dayton, Ohio. They provided me: One, with love. Two, the freedom to develop my skills. Three, a strong sense of values. Four, a high regard for education. I met my wife Donna, in 1973, and we were married six months later. With her I developed a stronger sense of responsibility and the fulfillment that comes with sharing our love. I am blessed with two wonderful children, who require me to set a strong example. All kids need heroes, not only mine, but every young child. This is especially important now when children are more vulnerable than during any other period in history. I hope I have 'touched' kids in a positive way. To me everyone who wears a uniform carries the responsibility of becoming a positive role model. When I think about, this is more important than any home run, any play, or any statistic. All these fade with time. But being a positive role model both on and off the field helps others become better human beings.

I'm thankful to baseball for many things. Perhaps the most important are the friendships it has given me. Playing baseball involves living with other players day in and day out - getting to know them, to learn from them, to lean on them in tough times, to survive together. I feel blessed to have made so many true friends in my seventeen years of wearing the Phillies uniform. The uniform of a first class organization rung throughout my career by two first class men: Ruly Carpenter and Bill Giles. I'm proud to call them both my friends. At times, I admit I can be a hard guy to get to know. This makes me even more grateful to those who invested their time and their trust to build a friendship with me. Each of you has my friendship forever.

And finally, my fans:

I want to tell you straight from the heart, how I feel about you and your influence on this game. As athletes, we're disciplined, we're focused, we're even tough. But I know of no athlete who is immune to fan reaction, positive or negative. Yes, you fans affect the game in a 'big' way. Calling Philadelphia fans spectators hardly describes your impact. You help mold the spirit of a team. Your positive feedback is crucial in the Phillies' right to stay on top. You know, I'm often asked what I miss the most about the game. It's tough to sort out all the wonderful memories and come up with a definite answer. But I can tell you this; I'll always miss the goose bumps I got when you cheered me. I've collected eighteen years of those goose bumps, from my first hit back in 1972 to the welcome you gave me tonight. To right now. That feeling can never be recreated, but that feeling will always be remembered.

My dreams started on a small playground near my home where I first learned how to hold a bat. My dreams came true here on this field. This game – baseball – is rich with strategy, talent, challenge, excitement and yes, tradition. But most of all, this game of baseball creates a bond – an indescribable bond, a bond that brings all of us together. All of us, not only teams but families, friends, communities and yes, even countries. At this very moment, I feel that bond and it will always be with me. I don't know where life will lead, but the Phillies and Philadelphia will forever hold a very special place in my heart.

I'll Take a "Triple" Scoop

When my daughter Nicole was about six-years old, I was the coach for her "T-pitch" baseball team. At this level, if a child is unable to hit the first two pitches that their own coach tosses to them, the ball is placed on the tee for them to hit. Quite obviously, kids are still learning the intracacies of the game at this age. Actor and director Rob Reiner was the coach for the other team. He was serving up "meatballs" that were getting hit pretty hard. The bases were loaded with nobody out. It looked like it was going to be another epic inning that would come to resemble a carousel in which the kids continued to go round and round the bases at will.

Reiner "fired" one in for the next batter, and the little boy hit a line drive directly at Nicole, who was playing first base at the time. She quickly thrust her glove up solely to protect her face and not get hurt. The ball found its way directly into the pocket of her glove for an out. She was elated that she had caught the ball, and by the roar of the crowd you would have thought she had just won the World Series.

Now, with the bases still loaded, not only the coaches but any parents with baseball instincts beyond those of a six-year-old yelled and hollered different instructions to players on both teams. Nicole innocently stepped on first base to record the second out to complete the double play, but she wasn't done yet. She ran across the infield toward her friend who was playing third base. The little guy who was the base runner on third base at the time of the hit had instinctively run on contact and was a few steps from touching home. My daughter, amongst the roars of all the parents, flipped the ball with an underhanded toss to her friend, who was still standing on third, to complete the triple play and end the game.

Most of the parents were still cheering in utter disbelief. On the car ride home after the game, Nicole innocently asked her brother, "Hey, what is a triple play?"

{Contributed by Michael Winegrad}

Ray King
[Major League Player]

*I**n the eighth round of the June 1995 free-agent draft, the Cincinnati Reds selected Ray King, the pride of Lambuth University in Jacksonville, Tennessee. After having played with six different teams in four years in the minors, King made his Major League debut in 1999 with the Chicago Cubs, and he made ten relief appearances before being sent back down to their AAA affiliate. He moved on to the Milwaukee Brewers organization in 2000, and in 2001, he had his breakout year in the big leagues under then Manager Davey Lopes' tutelage.*

I think it was the day that I got traded from the Chicago Cubs and was now headed over to the Milwaukee Brewers. When I walked into the Brewers' clubhouse, Davey Lopes and I had a conversation, and he pretty much said this is our situation "here's the ball and now it's your job to lose."

When I first heard Ray say it was "his job to lose," I didn't exactly understand what he meant. But when Ray continued to explain what Davey Lopes had said, it became evident to me why his manager's statement meant so much to the heralded reliever. He meant that after all the years King had spent in the minors working on his craft, he had finally earned the job and it was going to remain his job until he proved otherwise.

When a manager showed that much confidence in me, I thought, Wow, I have battled in the Minor Leagues for so long and finally got the respect of someone here. Now someone is giving me an opportunity. In this game, sometimes all it takes is getting an opportunity, and I remember going out there that first night knowing the job was mine no matter what happened! At that point, I started seeing things differently when I was out there pitching.

I saw the ball going in on a lefty before it happened. I saw myself getting the ground ball or two I needed, and right now I carry that confidence with me. The confidence that Davey showed in me helped get me where I am at today.

Now whatever may happen, if I don't stay in the Major Leagues, I know it is my fault because I have been given this opportunity. I still have that quote from Davey in my office at home: "It's your job to lose," and I look at every day as a reminder to go out and do my best!

Dmitri Young
[Major League Player]

Young was selected by the St. Louis Cardinals with the fourth overall pick in the first round of the 1991 June draft. As a member of the Cincinnati Reds, he hit a home run against Milwaukee's Jeff D'Amico on April 6th, 2001, the first home run hit in Miller Park. As a Detroit Tiger in 2003, Young joined the elite company of Willie Mays and Lou Gehrig when he became just the fourth player in Major League history to collect two triples and two home runs in one game.

The triple I hit in the playoffs on October 13, 1996 stands out for me. I was with the St. Louis Cardinals, and we were facing the Atlanta Braves in the 1996 League Championship Series. In Game 4 of that series, I was called upon to pinch hit against Denny Nagle. Bobby Cox didn't like that match-up and he took Nagle out of the game and brought in reliever Greg McMichaels to pitch to me. While this was going on, Ronny Gant came up to me and told me what to look for and how to hit against McMichaels. I ended up hitting a triple and driving in two runs, which put us ahead. We went on to win that game, putting us one game away from the World Series. Unfortunately for us, the 'real' Atlanta Braves showed up the next game and stomped us. But for a brief moment in time, when I hit that triple, it sure was electrifying inside Busch Stadium — and that moment still stands out in my mind.

Khalil Greene
[Major League Player]

While attending Clemson University, Greene was a four-time ACC Academic All-American and went on to win every major collegiate baseball player of the year award in his senior season, hitting .480 with 26 home runs and 86 RBIs and leading his team twice to the College World Series — in 2000 and again in 2002. These awards included the Golden Spikes Award, Atlantic Coast Conference Player of the Year, and Baseball America's College Player of the Year for 2002. In June of 2002, Greene became the second NCAA Division I player to reach the 400 career hit plateau. He was the 13th overall pick in the 2002 First-Year Player Draft and was named to the 2003 Major League Futures Game.

At this point in my career, I think three or four moments stick out more than any other. The first moment was when I was still playing in little league. I was about thirteen at the time and growing up in Key West, Florida. Our league was a real small little league, and we used to play the all-star games in different areas like Jacksonville and West Palm Beach. We played in an annual state tournament for several years, and we had never won until the year I was thirteen. Finally winning this tournament after being in it with the same group of guys for about five or six years was just a great feeling. At that time, winning as a team was all that we cared about —there was nothing individual about the way we played. We were more concerned about how we did as a team, which is baseball at its purest.

The second most memorable moment for me was when I was playing in the College World Series against Nebraska during my senior year at Clemson. They play the College World Series every year in Omaha, Nebraska, and about twenty-four thousand of the twenty-five thousand people in the stands were Nebraska fans. That was pretty wild, and we ended up winning in the bottom of the ninth to advance. *Greene hit a three-run homer and drove in five runs that game, and teammate Jeff Baker's RBI single in the bottom of the ninth drove in David Slevin for their remarkable comeback win.*

Since being here in the big leagues, my most memorable moment took place during a home game in San Diego against the Cubs in 2004. I made a few plays that night that gave me some recognition throughout the area and throughout the league. I take a lot of pride in my defense, and to make an impact defensively is difficult to do in this day and age. My defensive success that night was a culmination of a lot of things, so I would have to say that was a special moment for me as well. *Author's note: I was traveling around a series of ballparks with a friend of mine while I was working on this book. He and I were fortunate enough to be there at Petco Park in San Diego that particular evening to witness Khalil Greene's acrobatic and quite simply remarkable plays. He made three of the most incredible plays for a shortstop that I have ever witnessed. We couldn't wait to find a TV set to watch* SportsCenter *and see the replays over and over again. All three plays made* SportsCenter's *Top Ten Plays.*

Jorge Posada
[Major League Player]

*P*osada was selected by the New York Yankees in the twenty-fourth round of the June 1990 free-agent draft. The five-time American League All-Star catcher and two-time Silver Slugger Award winner has become one of the game's best catchers. Posada continues to anchor a pitching staff that has been to the playoffs every year since 1997.

The World Series championships—all four of them—are special, but individually, the perfect game with David Wells on May 17, 1998 was extra special because it is one of the toughest things you can accomplish between a pitcher and a catcher. Fortunately, I was able to be part of it. It was very exciting! We just got on the same page and didn't look back. As the game kept going along, he didn't need to shake me off because I was calling for the same pitch he wanted to throw. It was especially fun to be behind the plate that day, and being able to help him out was just a great experience for both of us.

Coco Crisp
[Major League Player]

Crisp is currently one of the most famous and successful alumni from the RBI (Reviving Baseball in Innercities) Program. He was taken by the St. Louis Cardinals in the 7th Round of the 1999 Major League Draft. In 2005, Crisp earned the starting leftfield spot for a Cleveland team that won 93 games while he hit .300, smacked 16 homeruns, and stole 15 bases and made several stellar defensive plays in the outfield.

My biggest experience before I made it to the Major Leagues was playing in the RBI Program when I was growing up. RBI allowed me to play when I wasn't getting the opportunity to play in high school. I was able to travel with the traveling teams and go places and get the chance to play in Major League stadiums at a young age. I was also able to compete in and win a RBI World Series tournament. Not only was the chance to play at a high level of competition early on big for me, and not only did it help me on the field, but RBI helped me in school because they had an educational program too. Playing in the 1995 RBI World Series in Seattle and winning that helped me a lot, but I have to admit that playing in the big leagues really takes the cake—to play at this level is a dream come true. When you really focus in and take the time to look around, to sit back and let it all sink in, you enjoy it even more.

Jim Edmonds
[Major League Player]

Edmonds was selected by the California Angels (now the Los Angeles Angels of Anaheim) in the 7th Round of the June 1988 free agent draft. The eight-time Gold-Glove centerfielder and five-time All-Star (once with the Angels in 1995 and four times with St. Louis 2000, 2003, 2004 and 2005) has become one of the most exciting players in the game today with his sensational glove play and his remarkable ability to pace one of the most potent lineups in recent history that included Albert Pujols, Scott Rolen and Reggie Sanders.

It is difficult to say what the most memorable experience has been because the whole situation is much more than I ever expected. It is really hard to say there is one moment that really sticks out, because I think every day that I get to play in the big leagues is more than I ever thought I would achieve.

One of the rewarding things about this occupation is you get to see a lot of remarkable things. I got to see Cal Ripken Jr. break Lou Gerhig's streak, Roger Clemens win his 300th game and also get his 4,000th strikeout, and I have seen a couple of pitchers throw no-hitters. I even saw a pitcher throw a perfect game! I have also had the chance to play in the playoffs (with the Cardinals in 2000 through 2002, and on to the World Series in 2004), which is one of the most unbelievable things ever. I have been very fortunate over the years and have had a lot of great things happen to me. I have been very lucky in my life, and everyday I play in the big leagues, it just blows me away.

Sean Casey
[Major League Player]

*C*asey *was selected by the Cleveland Indians in the second round of the June 1995 draft. He made his Major League debut against the Chicago White Sox at Comiskey Park, and he had a pinch hit single in the 9th inning off Jeff Darwin for his first Major League hit. Sean was later acquired by the Cincinnati Reds in a trade in 1998. In 1999, he became an All-Star in his first full season in the Major Leagues, hitting .332 with 42 doubles, 25 home runs, and 99 RBIs on the season.*

Watching Sean Casey on television doesn't do this gentleman justice in gauging his excitement and affable personality. I think that only by getting the opportunity to watch him in person at a ballgame or to meet him for a moment can one really get a feel for the energy that he can exude. He is one of the most effervescent and excitable individuals I have ever met. Working on this project allowed me a unique opportunity to go up and talk to a lot of "baseball people," but none treated me with more graciousness than Sean Casey. He truly is a big kid in a grown man's body, a man who loves the fact that one of his primary jobs in life is to play the game of baseball for a living.

I am originally from Pittsburgh and grew up going to a lot of games in Three River Stadium with my dad and my family. *After 30 years, Three Rivers Stadium, the former home of the Pittsburgh Steelers and Pirates, gave way to a new ballpark.* Fortunately, the Cincinnati Reds opened up against the Pirates in their new stadium, PNC Park, in 2001. Again, being from Pittsburgh, my whole family was there. I was really excited, and my first hit there, which was also my first at bat, was a home run! *It took place on Monday, April 9, 2001. Sean hit a two run homer in the top of the first in front of 36,954 fans and helped lead the Reds to an 8 to 2 victory over his hometown Pirates.* It was really something that my first hit there was a home run and it was the first home run at PNC Park.

Another awesome moment for me was at the All-Star game. I was able to take my son, Andrew, who was two-and-a- half at the time, with me on the field. We got him dressed up in a Cincinnati Reds uniform, and I took him out there with me and was able to share that moment with him. We could see my wife in the stands, and she was with my dad and our family—it's one of the experiences that I'll never forget. It was priceless!

Mark Mulder
[*Major League Player*]

After attending Michigan State and being named the team's Most Valuable Player in 1997 and 1998, Mulder was the second player chosen overall in the June 1998 draft. In 2001, he finished second in the American League Cy Young Award, behind the New York Yankees' Roger Clemens, after winning 21 games for the Oakland Athletics. Within the three seasons between 2001 and 2003, Mulder won more games than any pitcher in Major League Baseball, including the likes of Curt Shilling, Mike Mussina, Randy Johnson and Roger Clemens.

I think my most memorable experience is my first big league start on April 18th, 2000 against Cleveland. They had that great lineup in 2000 – Vizquel, Alomar, Ramirez, Thome, Sexson, Justice, Alomar Jr., etc—and we ended up winning 8 to 5. I ended up giving up four runs that day in six innings and got the win. It was awesome, and to this day I think that is why I love playing in that park (Jacobs Field). *After giving up a home run to Manny Ramirez in the first inning, Mulder settled in and ended up striking out six Indians in route to picking up his first Major League win in as many tries.*

Another favorite memory was winning Game 1 in the 2001 Playoffs against the Yankees and then starting again in Game 5. As I threw the first pitch up there I was numb. I couldn't even feel my body. It was just so awesome, and winning that game just made the experience that much more fun. Those are two more of my memorable moments—just being out there and playing.

Playing with Barry Zito and Tim Hudson was amazing. We're best friends. We were in the minors together and when we each struggled it was tough, because you didn't want to go up to one of them and tell him you're not doing this or that. For example, I was giving up some more walks than I had been and I talked with Barry for about thirty minutes about what I was thinking at the time and what my approach was. I have said this before and they have said the same thing, I would not be the pitcher that I am today if I didn't have them as teammates the past couple of years because they made me better. With the three of us, we pushed each other so much. If Huddy threw a three hit shutout, I wanted to throw a two hit shutout, and if I threw a two hit shutout, Zito wanted to throw a one hit shutout. It's not to outdo the other person, it's just that we pushed each other to be better. I think that is how Rich (Harden) was able to develop so quickly since he is still so young. When people asked us, who of us three had the best stuff, we would say it's none of us…It's Rich. That is awesome to see him doing so well. It was not just about the three of us, it was about a team.

Mr. Clutch

I went to Regis University in Denver, Colorado, which does not have the best climate for baseball. We had a double header scheduled with the University of Wyoming, and it was as cold as any day that I can remember ever playing baseball. It was snowing off and on by the time we reached Laramie, Wyoming, but not enough to cancel the game. It was also free batting helmet night at the stadium, so every kid in Laramie was at the game.

My knee was messed up that season due to a reconstructive surgery, but I was still available to pinch hit if they needed me. Well, the first game was in the ninth inning and they were up 1 to 0. The game had taken a long time and it was getting colder, so the coaches decided not to play the second game that night but to reschedule it for later in the season. My best buddy, Mass, stepped to the plate and proceeded to hit the furthest ball I have ever seen. I'm not kidding — it was 550 feet if it was an inch. He was so jazzed that, as he watched the ball clear the telephone wires in left, he lost track of the baseline and almost ran directly into our dugout. We then went through the tenth and then the eleventh with no more scoring. Mass led off the eleventh. He walked and then stole second base. The next two hitters grounded out and didn't advance him.

The coach then called me in as a pinch hitter. I hadn't even taken batting practice that day and had been sitting on the ice cold bench all game. I had to run back into the clubhouse to find my jersey and then find my knee brace. I was struggling to put both of them on as I walked out towards the batters box. I hit left handed, so it was a short walk from the on-deck circle. I took a couple of practice swings and stepped up to the plate. The pitcher was a short reliever and was throwing in the low-to mid-nineties, which seems much faster than that at 25 degrees. The first pitch was a high fastball, and my swing was so late that the ball was in the glove as the bat left my shoulder. I called time out and shook myself. I figured the dude was going to bring heat again and go for an easy one-two-three pitch strike out. This time, I stepped back in the box and the guy brought the high heat again. Instead of trying to kill the ball, I just made contact and drove it in to shallow left center, scoring Mass from second base. I then rounded first, came back to the base, called time out, and asked for a pinch runner. I limped back to the dugout, and the whole team was going nuts. We held them in the bottom half of the inning and won the game. All of the kids with their new University of Wyoming batting helmets were bummed out to say the least.

{Contributed by Jimmy Marsh}

I Don't Care If I Ever Get Back

Another one of my all-time favorite memories is one that happened in the fall of 1998 when I was working with the San Diego Padres. As you may recall, it was a magical season in baseball that year, with Sammy Sosa and Mark McGwire packing stadiums with fans in record numbers as they looked to break Roger Maris' single season home run record. It just so happened that Sammy Sosa and the Chicago Cubs were scheduled to start wrapping up their season in sunny San Diego, still looking to claim the National League Wild Card slot in the playoffs.

Being from Chicago, I was entirely caught up in the fact that the Cubbies, America's lovable losers of the 20th Century, had a legitimate shot at the playoffs and were coming in to take on my employers, the San Diego Padres. I had requested the day off to watch the first game of the four game series, and in eager anticipation, I couldn't sit still for more than a half an hour the entire day. I figured the best thing for me to do would be to head off to my sanctuary — the ol' ballpark. I got there pretty early for the game, *about five hours early* actually. I think it is safe to say that most people would consider getting there that many hours before the first pitch going overboard, and maybe even a little insane. But I didn't think so, since I was a Padre employee and could walk right up to the stadium and go have lunch in any seat I wanted, box or bleacher. Many people will tell you that they find it relaxing to go to a park to get some fresh air and eat their lunch, and I am the same way, but *my* park just happens to have a pitcher's mound, a couple of dugouts, and a scoreboard.

As I sat alone with a slice of pizza and with my feet up on the railing above the visiting dugout in Qualcomm Stadium, decked out in my Cubs jersey, floppy hat, kaki shorts and pair of flip flops, Rob Fukuzaki (Los Angeles based ABC sports anchor) walked onto the field and saw me eating my " pre-game meal." He questioned how in the world I was able to get into the ballpark past heavy security that early and without any sign of a press credential any where! I simply informed him that I worked for the Padres but was from Chicago and a devout Cubs fan. He took the bait and asked if he could interview me. Being the horribly vain person that I am, I gladly obliged, praying that someone I knew would see me on TV so that I could prove this actually happened. I joined Rob on the field for the interview. At the time, I knew I had no business being on the field to do the interview and could have easily done it from the first row of seats, but I also knew (well, *hoped* is a better word) that with the media circus taking place surrounding this game I would be able to blend in — and if I just played it cool I might be able to see some of my heroes up close. I couldn't believe it!! There I was getting interviewed by an ABC announcer on a live TV feed that went out to Chicago, Los Angeles and San Diego stations. I don't remember exactly what questions he asked me let alone how I responded. The whole experience was just a blur because of the huge adrenaline rush I was suffering due to my surroundings. Just after the interview was over, I was standing around talking with Rob when a couple of my friends called me to tell me that they saw me on TV with the Chicago Cubs filing onto the field behind me and then warming up before the game. Being the responsible employee of the San Diego Padres, I knew full well that I should start making my way up to my seat, and I did what most people would do — *I stayed on the field and started talking to a few of the players.* Then a few more. Then a few more. It finally got to the point that I was playing catch with a few of the Cubs. I had the opportunity to talk with a couple of Chicago Cubs legends like Ron Santo and Billy Williams and was completely swept up in the moment.

Then, as I thought it couldn't get much better, I heard my name being hollered, by not one, but two people at once. Thinking someone wanted my autograph after my appearance on television, I looked over to see who the lucky winners of the Steve Sullivan autograph sweepstakes would be. *Both of my supervisors* were there to greet me in unison with the wonderful news that, from that point on, my service with the ball club was no longer needed. Much like you read on the sports pages and hear on *SportsCenter* nowadays, this was purely a "business decision" for the Padres and I realized they were simply allowing me test out the "free agent waters." I didn't mind all that much, since I still had my tickets for the rest of the four-game series and could now cheer on my beloved Cubs as they attempted to make the playoffs without being on the schedule to work for the remaining games.

I had quite a few interesting messages on my answering machine when I got home because the live interview was broadcast in Chicago too. A couple of disbelieving family members and friends saw the fateful interview and cracked up whole heartedly when I told them that I was "released from my contract" by the San Diego Padres shortly after my first interview.

{Contributed by Steve Sullivan}

Mom, Are You Kidding Me?

I grew up in what you might call a "baseball family." In fact, when my father passed away, they named the Babe Ruth League that he had been involved with for many years the "Pete Janin Babe Ruth League." Both of my sons have grown up playing baseball, and each spring I look forward to the beginning of a new season. I find watching a ballgame on television is a great way to spend an evening after a stressful day at the office. In a few words: I love baseball. I have watched my kids play since they started in T-ball, when they couldn't even hit the ball off a tee and would swing so hard that when they missed they totally turned themselves around. This is one of my funnier baseball moments and involves me and one of my sons, John. Well, sort of indirectly.

I had to travel to Seattle, Washington for a few days on a business trip. When I got on the elevator one morning, there was a very nice looking man already aboard and we proceeded to strike up a friendly conversation. Upon arriving at the lobby, we wished each other a good day, and he then approached a group of men in the lobby who greeted him as Cal. I knew it! I knew he looked familiar! It was Cal Ripken Jr., and the men who greeted him were a few of his teammates from the Baltimore Orioles. They were in town to play the Seattle Mariners. I couldn't believe it! I had missed a golden opportunity to ask him for his autograph for my son, who of course would have thought I was the most wonderful mom in the world.

To say the least, I did not tell John about my encounter in Seattle with Mr. Ripken, but I relayed what had happened to a friend when I thought John was out of hearing distance. Upon hearing the whole story, John came flying into the room in total disbelief that I, his mom and a huge baseball fan, did not recognize Cal Ripken Jr. All I could muster in my own defense was that Ripkin was not in his uniform and therefore didn't have his name on his back so I didn't recognize him. I acknowledged the fact that I totally blew it by not asking for his autograph! But by this point, John left the room shaking his head in utter disbelief.

{Contributed by Jaime Janin}

Happy Father's Day

It was a cool, gray, damp, cloudy day in Chicago. "November?" you might ask. Nope, it was August 11, 2004 at Wrigley Field, a day that I am sure I'll never forget.

You see, my stepson had been telling me earlier in the year about having the opportunity to be on the field and to meet some players while in Florida during Spring Training. Apparently, teams are a lot less strict about access then compared to the regular season. His vivid account suddenly caused me to say something like, "Wow, I wish I could have been with you. I wish I could walk out onto a baseball field and meet some of the players." At the time, I thought that was as far as it would go, but then Father's Day (June 20, 2004) came around. My stepson surprised me with tickets for us to attend the "Meet the Cubs and Have a Ball" event. This was a special event that the Chicago Cubs offered, with the proceeds going to the their Cubs Care charity.

His mom and I had only been married a little over a year, and he and I had a great relationship already, but needless to say, I was blown away by his generosity. When I told him, "Thanks, but it's too much," he said, "I love you and I wanted your wish to come true." My wish to be able to walk out onto a baseball field and meet the players was about to be fulfilled. The day started out grey and damp but wound up being one of the best days of my entire life, one that I couldn't have imagined beforehand and will never forget.

We were given a baseball as we entered Wrigley Field, and we were two of only 300 people who were able to talk to and get autographs from the manager, Dusty Baker, all the coaches and all of the players (except for the pitcher who was going to start the game that night). I even got a personal introduction to some of the guys my stepson had met previously.

Imagine being up close and personal with all the big-time stars on the team, including Sammy Sosa, Nomar Garciaparra, Kerry Wood. Imagine being personally introduced to wonderful guys like Derrek Lee, Todd Walker, and Mark Prior by your stepson. We were then allowed onto the field and given cameras. We had noticed that they were putting out names up on the giant centerfield scoreboard. We both took pictures of each other on the field and of the scoreboard with our names in letters at least two feet tall —how cool is that?

The "Meet the Cubs and Have a Ball" event didn't include seats to that night's SOLD OUT game, but somehow my stepson had managed to buy club box seat tickets ten rows from the field, and no, not from a scalper but from the Wrigley Field box office a couple of hours before the first pitch. It was as if it were meant to be—we were destined to have great seats for this game and the experience was magical! The icing on the cake was a great 5 to 1 Cubs win. The terms *thank you* and *I love you* don't begin to tell this great young man how special I feel and how I'll never forget our "Father's Day" celebration.

{Contributed by Paul Pruett}

Mark Prior
[*Major League Player*]

The Chicago Cubs chose Prior with the second pick overall in the 2001 draft after his remarkable junior season at the University of Southern California. In his first full year in the Major Leagues, he was an integral component in the Cubs' pitching staff and helped lead the team to the National League Central Division title, was selected to the National League All-Star team, and finished with an 18 win season and a 2.43 ERA.

I think the most memorable moment for me is being in the playoffs in 2003. It was the first time that the Cubs had been in the playoffs in a while, and to win that first playoff series, in I don't know how long, was special. It was especially memorable being able to pitch against the Braves in the incredible atmosphere here at Wrigley Field. The fans were great and it was such an intense ballgame. It was also my chance to go up against a great lineup that I hadn't pitched well against earlier in the year, to try to help us by getting the 2 to 1 advantage.

Before that all important game, Mark was 0 and 2 lifetime against the Atlanta Braves with a 6.35 ERA, but on that September night he was not to be denied, pitching a playoff masterpiece, a complete game while allowing only two hits, one run and striking out seven Braves.

Phil Nevin
[Major League Player]

A member of the 1992 U.S. Olympic Team that played in Barcelona, Spain, Nevin was selected by the Houston Astros with the overall number one pick in the draft. He had an All-American career at Cal State-Fullerton and was the recipient of the 1992 Golden Spikes Award, which goes to the top amateur baseball player of the year, after hitting .402 with 22 home runs and 86 RBIs. Nevin was named the 1992 College World Series MVP despite the Titans' elimination in the Championship game. After starting the season with the Astros AAA affiliate, all of his hard work paid off on June 11, 1995 when he got his first chance to play in a big league game.

I would say that the first time I put on a Major League uniform really stands out for me. Getting called up and then getting my first at bat, just the whole thing is awesome. The experience of playing in the Major Leagues for the first time goes by so quickly, but it is the day that you never forget. I was in the Houston Astros system when I got the call. I took a six o'clock flight, and I flew through the night and wasn't able to sleep at all. I remember we had a one o'clock game in Houston against the Cincinnati Reds. I didn't have any plays (balls hit to me) in the field, but for my first at bat they had just intentionally walked Jeff Bagwell to get to me. I got a base hit off C.J. Nitkowski and drove in a run. That moment for sure really stands out for me.

*Every time I hold a ball in my hand and put that suit on
that's been my biggest day.*
-Dizzy Dean
Hall of Fame Pitcher

One-Two-Three Strikes Your Out at the Ol' Ballgame

B aseball has always been a big part of my life. When I went away to college, I didn't know what I wanted to do with my life, but ultimately, I decided I should probably get involved with something I enjoy. Baseball was my easy answer. I set up a major in the sports business field, and for three summers I interned with the Brooklyn Cyclones, a farm team of the New York Mets. During my spring semester of my senior year, I landed an internship with the Aberdeen IronBirds, a farm club of the Orioles. While interning, a fulltime position opened up, and I landed the job. I was to start eight days after graduation.

Most of my friends graduated, took a few months off, and began work the first week of August. They thought *they* jumped right in, but the beginning of August was the beginning of my third full month of work, and the second half of our short season. Even before my friends had started their jobs, I had seen professional baseball history made in our very own park and by one of our very own players.

Wednesday, June 23rd seemed like a nice enough night for a ballgame. The sky was fairly clear, the air late-spring warm, and the IronBirds were off to a 4 to 1 start. Our starting pitcher that night, Luis Ramirez, was making his second start of the year, following a no-decision on Opening Day, a game Aberdeen won in extra innings. When I was putting the media guide together before the season, Ramirez' numbers in rookie ball in 2003 stood out. He had a good ERA, and exceptional control and strikeout numbers. Maybe we were missing something, but he didn't look dominant in his first start, at least on the radar gun. He wasn't dominant in his second start, either, but that was the case ONLY on the radar gun.

At about 7:07, Ramirez let loose with the game's first pitch —a called strike. We would see plenty more of those the rest of the night, in fact, 57 more strikes in just 75 pitches. Jamestown's leadoff batter grounded out to short, the last out recorded by an Aberdeen fielder until the 6th inning. Ramirez sent the number two hitter in the Jammers' lineup down looking. Their number three hitter at least went down with a fight, swinging at and missing a 91 mph fastball that was two-thirds of the way between the belt and the letters and over the heart of the plate. After a half inning, Luis Ramirez had struck out two batters. The next ten Jamestown batters were about to suffer the same fate.

"He's not throwing that hard or with that much movement," someone said in the press box in between innings. While most press boxes are pretty stuffy and quiet, the IronBirds have both their video production and media relations staffs in the same large room, which means that there are some loud moments during exciting games and gives the press box the same lively feel as the rest of the sold out stadium. Cheering has, admittedly, happened more times than ideal from the vantage of the guys upstairs, but that makes you feel like you are watching the game with your friends instead of just doing a job without enjoyment. "He looks good though. They aren't picking him up," someone else said from another part of the press box. That turned out to be the understatement of the year.

In the top of the second, Ramirez continued where he left off, throwing mostly first pitch strikes. He sat the cleanup hitter, who was leading off the second, down looking with one of a handful of changeups thrown on the evening. The number five hitter went down swinging, but when the ball escaped catcher

Whit Pierce's grasp, the runner took off for first, and he reached when first baseman Mike Costello dropped Pierce's throw. "Good," I thought. "Now he can strikeout four this inning." But I only half meant it. To help confirm my psychic abilities, Ramirez sat down batters six and seven in the Jamestown lineup, both swinging at his suddenly unhittable 89-92 mph chest-high fastball over the middle of the plate. "Six in a row," I called out, and the buzz started for the first time in the press box.

The IronBirds came up and went down quickly in the bottom half of the second, and I checked in our radio booth to see how the night was going. "Luis looks great," Steve Melewski, our broadcaster, said. "He's gonna keep this up," he added confidently. I was just hoping to see another early season win, and at best, a new team record. Perusing the media guide, I saw that, in our first year, John Maine had struck out ten straight batters over the course of two appearances. The team record for strikeouts by a pitcher in one game was also at ten. "Steve," I said. "If he takes down the side in order this inning, we're going to be on the verge of dealing with some pretty big baseball news here."

Of course you could guess what had to happen in the third, as batters eight, nine and one all went down — the first two swinging and the last looking at the first curveball of the night — via strikeouts. The press box was suddenly jumping. "What's the record for consecutive K's in a game?" I thought to myself. After my years of baseball watching, card collecting and general useless trivia knowledge, I had an inkling that my Mets and Tom Terrific had something to do with the record, but I didn't recall the exact numbers. I hopped on one of the open press box computers and started checking Google, *Baseball Reference, Baseball Almanac* and anything else I could think of. All baseball records are stored, but the quirky ones are sometimes harder to find, especially the Minor League records. The Major League record for consecutive batters

K'd is in fact ten, and the record was set by Tom Seaver in 1970. With Ramirez at nine in a row, and the Jamestown hitters looking clueless, I sensed that we just needed a little luck and we could have a pretty terrific story on our hands.

In the Aberdeen half of the third, I ran down to the office to see if we had any record books for the New York-Penn League, Minor League Baseball, anything. We didn't, but IronBirds General Manager Jeff Eiseman was in the press box during the game and gave me some contacts to call if the K's continued in the fourth. Of course, they did.

Leading off the fourth for Jamestown was their number two hitter, shortstop Jon Fulton. Fulton had been Ramirez' first victim of the night, and in his second at bat, he went down again, although this time he left with some dignity, swinging right through that chest-high fastball instead of watching it go by. Fulton was strikeout number ten, and there was a mini eruption in the press box. Steve did a great job relaying what had happened to the listeners at home, even announcing the tied team records. I figured another strikeout, two more max, and we might have baseball history. Luis kept on rolling, punching out the three and four hitters in the Jamestown lineup for a second time! Through four innings, he had struck out twelve batters — all consecutively after the leadoff groundout thanks to the dropped third strike — and he had not given up a hit. The crowd was buzzing in amazement at what was unfolding before their eyes.

I burned the phones almost immediately. This was only my fourth game at this job, and I already had a potential story of a lifetime. The adrenaline was flowing, and I was doing all I could to verify what I thought was happening right before my very eyes. My first call was to Dave Chase, GM of the Memphis Redbirds, the AAA Affiliate of the St. Louis Cardinals. Dave is also a Minor League Baseball historian, and if anyone could help out, he would be the guy. There was no answer, but I left a message. I figured in a worst case scenario he would be able to confirm our "record" one way or another by the next morning.

I went back online and found Minor League Baseball's phone number. No one was there that time of day. My next call went to the Baseball Hall of Fame, but they had nothing to help me out. I looked for a Minor League Baseball Hall of Fame contact, but such a place does not yet exist. I ran back down to the office to look for any type of league record book for a second time. I rifled through everything, papers on desks, books anywhere we had them, and came up with nothing.

While I was downstairs, the IronBirds scored three runs, staking Ramirez to a three to nothing lead. First baseman Mike Costello atoned for his earlier error by singling in a run. He came around to score when third baseman Rob Marconi laced a two RBI triple, giving Ramirez what looked like all the support he would need. As I was being filled in on the runs scored while Ramirez was warming up for the fifth, I realized the streak was still going. With his pitch count set by the coaching staff at around 75 early in the season, it looked like this would be Ramirez' last inning. The only thing I could think of was more strikeouts, for Luis to really blow the record away, whatever it was, for we still had no confirmation at that point. The Jamestown third baseman put an end to that thought by actually making contact with a fastball and dropping a blooper into short centerfield on a 1-1 count. Arturo Rivas was playing normal depth centerfield, and when he dove to try to make the catch, the ball bounced over and a little behind him, allowing the runner to go to second. Everyone in the press box stood and clapped for Ramirez, while the crowd did the same. We did not know exactly what we had witnessed, just that it seemed pretty extraordinary.

Ramirez "settled down" after giving up the leadoff double, and he struck out the next three batters to end the top of the fifth. His final line for the day (he was pulled for pitch count after the fifth inning): 5 IP, 0 R, 1 H, 0 BB, 15 K, 76 pitches/58 strikes. His line looked as ridiculous as the Jamestown batters waving helplessly at his 90 mph fastball.

As the game stretched into its second half, I continued to focus on how to find the historical context to Ramirez' accomplishment. I continued looking on every baseball website I could think of, still feeling the adrenaline. My best efforts could only uncover the MLB record. Just taking an educated guess, I figured Luis had at least tied the Minor League record, although I truly had nothing to base that supposition on. I ran back down towards our offices, and in the seventh inning—the IronBirds were now down 6 to 3 as the seventh inning stretch was underway I began pumping out a press release. I wanted to word it correctly. I was unsure of the accomplishment's status as a record, but I still wanted to grab the media's attention because it was a tremendous story—and possibly something never before done in baseball history.

I finished up and faxed it out between 9 and 9:30, as the game was headed towards the ninth. At that point, the story was out there and whoever found it interesting could contact us while the game finished up and the post game commenced. The ninth inning went pretty quickly, and after printing out box scores, I headed to the home clubhouse with the local media. Right before we got there, my cell phone started ringing. The AP had grabbed the story and wanted to run with it. I told them I was waiting word of whether or not Ramirez' performance was a record, so they said it would be a good idea to follow up the next day when I found out one way or another. It seemed like a good idea, but I was still so excited that I wanted finality right then and there. I told them I would definitely get in touch tomorrow and hopefully with some good news.

The local guys talked to Ramirez' catcher, Whit Pierce, and our pitching coach, Andre Rabouin. The accomplishment was hard to explain because most people couldn't understand one of the most basic questions: how did he do it? He wasn't overpowering, and he wasn't throwing anything tricky or deceptive, so how was it possible to strike out twelve straight batters? Ramirez couldn't explain what the batters saw, just what he did and how proud he was of his accomplishment. He talked about his fastball and his easy delivery and working in a few off-speed pitches. The thing he said that stood out most was that he thought he felt strong, like he could have thrown all night.

Almost two and a half hours after he left the game, I couldn't get over just how easy Ramirez made it look that night. The baseball fan in me was ready to stand and clap on every two-strike count during the game, and while our crowd was abuzz with the events, they weren't making Ramirez reach down for something extra. Throwing free and easy without the slightest look of strain or stress on his face, Ramirez just smoothly rolled the ball off his fingers, and pretty much right by every Jamestown batter who stood in his path. Not only was his outing easy on the eyes, it was potentially something that had never been done in the history of professional baseball — in over 150 years!.

I finished up for the night and got a few more calls, but none from Dave Chase. The excitement caught up to me on the drive home and started to knock me out. By the time I got home, the adrenaline had worn off completely, and I fell asleep as soon as my head hit the pillow.

I woke up on Thursday hoping for the best, but I was also half-expecting to still be in limbo. A little while after I got to work, Dave and someone from Minor League Baseball had both called. Dave let me know that, of all the league record books he had, ten was the previous listed record for consecutive strikeouts in a game.

That bit of news woke me up very quickly, and my eyes felt like they were bugging out of my head. I thanked him, put together a news release, and called everyone who I hoped would run with the story.

I told our staff and coaches that day that Luis had in fact set a record the previous night. Everyone was excited, especially the players. Luis was very happy for his record, but disappointed the team couldn't nail down the win.

The story was picked up by many major publications and many local newspapers across the country. Once it hit the AP ticker, it spread like wildfire. Luis became a hot interview prospect, and he was interviewed by the *Washington Post* and other area papers. His accomplishment was huge, and every time he pitched the rest of the year, our crowds — and the road crowds from what I was told—could only talk about his start against Jamestown. They had come to see for themselves just how great a pitcher this man was.

All in all, it was an action-packed 24 hours, with steadily growing excitement and a fantastic end result. All records are made to be broken, and in all probability, one day Luis Ramirez will no longer have the record for consecutive strikeouts in a game. Whoever breaks that record will certainly deserve it, and everyone associated with it will hopefully enjoy it as much as the IronBirds and the staff did.

{Contributed by Jay Moskowitz}

W hile I was in the process of completing this book, I spoke frequently with a few of my friends about some of their baseball experiences, especially those they considered the most outstanding moments they had when involved with the game—as a player or a fan. In one of these conversations with an otherwise shy and extremely humble friend, I was treated to two of his most memorable moments in the game, and in fact, his stories are quite remarkable as you will soon see.

What I discovered was that he had accomplished a couple of feats that only a few players in the history of professional or collegiate baseball had ever achieved. The next two stories reveal how astonishing the accomplishments were.

During one particular series against Air Force, Spencer Oborn was in what one could call the zone. This took place during his sophomore campaign while he was still at Brigham Young University, before he transferred to Cal State Fullerton for his junior season.

Spencer Oborn hit for a second cycle in as many days, and he nearly pulled off a third in three games as BYU swept the Air Force Academy. Oborn hit for his first cycle on a Friday afternoon, leading BYU to a 26-6 victory. Oborn started his hot streak with a bunt single and a sacrifice fly in a ten-run first inning, hit a double in the third, a triple in the fourth, a three-run homer in the fifth, and finished the day with a solo homer in the eighth inning.

During the second game of the series the next day, Oborn led off with a triple to right field in the first inning, and he followed up with a two-run homer in the second, a three-run homer and a double in the fourth, and then hit a single in the sixth inning to go five for five with six RBIs in the 20-8 victory over the demoralized Air Force Academy.

In the third and final game of the series, BYU beat Air Force 26-4, and Oborn didn't let up. He continued to swing a hot bat, singling in his first at bat and following that with doubles in the second and third innings, a two-run homer in the fifth, and a run-scoring single in the seventh. He fell a triple short of three consecutive games with a cycle when he grounded into a fielder's choice in his final at-bat in the eighth inning, thus putting a halt to his amazing run of consecutive games with a cycle. His unbelievable week consisted of a streak with eleven consecutive hits, a .741 batting average, and this series increased his overall season average from .364 to .420, raised his slugging percentage to 1.087 and his total bases on the year to fifty.

After reading the second story about Spencer Oborn, you'll also see why the Chicago White Sox drafted the 6'3" right-handed hitting outfielder (as the 429th player chosen) in the 14th round of the 1999 June draft, between Albert Pujols (402nd) and Jake Peavy (472nd) and ahead of Lyle Overbay in the 18th Round (538th).

Standing Strong at 37

All records and streaks in the game of baseball are nothing short of miraculous. Consider batting: a hitter could do everything in his power perfectly and still fail. Even the greatest hitters in baseball history "fail" about seven times in ten. That is what makes the streak that I had in 1999 after transferring to Cal State Fullerton from BYU so unbelievable to me. Like most every member of every team, we began the baseball season with high hopes of having a wonderful year. My season began innocently enough. I went 0 for 2 in my only two at bats against the Stanford Cardinal. The next night, however, it all began for me with my first hit as a Titan.

After I got my first hit under my belt, I was just hoping to get a chance to play and help the team win. After about a month into the season, I still remember being in the locker room with my teammate Aaron Rifkin, and I commented to him that I thought I had a base hit in every game so far other than the first game of the year. We both thought about it for a couple of seconds, then after going through the season in our minds, we agreed this seemed to be the case. We concluded that, if in fact we were right, this feat would be a nice accomplishment.

Soon after our private conversation, we had our suspicions confirmed when there was a story about my growing streak in the local newspaper. This is where some of the speculation started about whether or not I might be able to catch Robin Ventura's fifty-eight game hitting streak record set in 1987 when he played for Oklahoma State

During my hitting streak, I definitely felt quite a bit of tension and a higher level of stress as the expectation levels continued to mount. One Sunday afternoon game at the University of Pacific in Stockton, California stands out in my mind. My hitting streak had been written about in the sports section of several newspapers for a couple of weeks, and here we were, facing the University of Pacific in the top of the ninth inning and I was without a hit. I remember being on deck, surveying the crowd and looking towards my mom. I could tell that she was nervous. My dad, who would wander around every stadium because he couldn't sit still, was in a different part of the stadium, as usual, but the concentrated look on his face told me he was nervous as well. For me, that was the first moment that I thought there might be something special about what was happening with my streak. Before that moment, I saw the streak as more of an aberration that was, of course, going to end soon. But as I walked to home plate and started to dig into the batters box this time, I felt my adrenaline kick in. As the ball left the bat and I saw that I had singled to left, I let out a sigh of relief and thought to myself, "I don't ever want to wait until the ninth inning again!"

The people who play baseball are a very superstitious lot. If a pitcher is throwing a no hitter, no one will talk to him because it might bring him bad luck or take him out of "the zone." During batting practice of a mid-week game against Loyola Marymount, my head coach at Cal State Fullerton, Coach Horton, was talking with Loyola Marymount's Coach Cruz. As I was jogging back to the outfield and passing by the two coaches, Coach Horton called me over, and as I made my way over to them, Coach Horton nodded his head in Coach Cruz's direction. As I glanced over at Coach Cruz, he said with a big smile, "I hear you have a good hitting streak going." Knowing full well what he was trying to do, I just smiled back and said, "Yes." He said, "Good luck with that." As I jogged away I could hear both coaches chuckling.

In the bottom of the first inning, I hit a triple down the right field line, and after I slid into third and brushed away some of the loose dirt, I looked into our dugout where Coach Horton was looking into Loyola's dugout and smiling at Coach Cruz like a proud father.

As the season wore on, the hitting streak became a big joke within the locker room amongst the whole team. We could pull out a big win, and maybe one of my teammates would even have a huge game, going four-for-four, but all anyone was interested in was if I got a hit. It seemed like there were only two questions the media wanted to ask: Did the Titans win? And did Oborn get a hit?

On a memorable Friday night towards the end of the season, Titan fans filled the stadium for a game that would normally draw about 800 fans but instead drew over 1,500 people. With all the buzz swirling within the stands, it was no secret why these people were there. I continued to approach this game as I had all the rest, however, I still had a couple of my superstitions in place: the piece of tape on the sleeve of my undershirt the trainers called my "hit diamond" and my father wearing his familiar Titan hat and standing in his "lucky" spot — leaning against the light pole that was just above our third-base dugout.

Every time I walked up to home plate, the crowd applauded loudly. I could practically feel the crowd willing me toward the record. As I came up for my fourth at bat in the bottom of the seventh inning with the game under control, I was without a hit. Now, this situation had happened a couple of times before, and somehow, someway, I found a way to squeak a ball through the infield for the hit that kept the streak alive. But this time was different—this time there were actually people rooting and cheering for me to pull this off. I remember thinking to myself as I walked to the plate, "This is it. Let's do it!" After I grounded out and was trotting back to the dugout, the crowd cheered and I thought to myself, "It was a nice run."

Just as I got to the dugout and was receiving high fives from my teammates, I heard, "Let's get him another chance. Let's bat around and get him up again." At that moment, as I looked at all of my teammates, I knew I was going to get another chance. Sure enough, in the bottom of the eighth inning and with two outs, my teammates had come through and given me another opportunity. Now this was *really* it! Barring a miraculous comeback, this was going to be my last chance to keep the streak alive. I knew that I was going to get a hit. How could I *not* get a hit after the stars had been aligned for so many games in a row, and now, as if the stars had aligned once more, getting another chance because my teammates battled and made this happen. It was destiny.

As I walked to the plate, there was again the hopeful and supportive cheering from the fans. I could somehow feel that everyone in the park, excluding the other team, wanted me to get a hit. Now there is no feeling in the world like having that many people pulling for you to succeed. I cannot put into words how this felt. As good as this feeling was though, after a few quick pitches, it was all over with a weak ground ball to the first baseman.

I ran as fast as I could to beat the first baseman, but he had touched the base before I could get anywhere near it. I could hear the crowd sigh collectively. They knew now that this streak had come to an end. I stood near first for a brief moment, knowing that I had failed. I handed my helmet to Coach Kirby, who patted me on the back and said, "Great job." At that moment, the crowd was standing and cheering as I jogged out to left field with a big smile on my face. As I ran past teammates, they all yelled, "Nice job O.B.!"

I settled into left field at the top of the ninth inning wondering what might have been. With only one out to go in the game, Coach Horton came out of the dugout and signaled for me to come in, and I saw a teammate running out toward me. I really did not know what exactly to do, so I started to jog in. As I reached the infield, the rest of my teammates all came out of the dugout to give me congratulatory hugs and pats on the back. The crowd was still there, and everyone was on their feet clapping and cheering. There are no words to describe how I felt at that moment, but I can tell you that I will never forget how I felt that day. I have never been so proud of any game in which I played than I am of that game in which I went 0 for 4.

{Contributed by Spencer Oborn}

Take Me Out to the Ballgame

As a young girl, I soon learned that baseball was something that my dad and brothers "watched" on our black and white television whenever they could. I say "watched" loosely because they all yelled and screamed, swore and cheered towards one another or in unison when a big play took place. Personally, I ignored those games, and my brothers' and my dad's noise. It seemed like they could talk forever, or so it seemed to me, about people none of them I really knew, people I had never heard of before, and about numbers that made no sense to me.

Well, many years later, I realized I should have paid attention because now my toddler was glued to the TV "watching" baseball. I couldn't believe how animated his reactions were for someone so young. He was reading the sports page by the age of four, so he could talk with my neighbor about baseball.

I knew that I'd better try to learn more about the game. Somehow it was in his genes, what made him tick, and I gained a newfound appreciation for the enthusiasm my dad and brothers had for this so-called game. At the age of six, my son couldn't wait to put on his uniform, and he would wear it any chance he could. A whole new world opened up to me, and a very strong bond developed between a mom and her son.

Whenever I think of baseball, I think of all the times I "bribed" a ten-or eleven-year-old to help me clean up around the house on a nice sunny Saturday morning in the summer or early fall. I used to pop in Neil Diamond in the eight-track player and "make him a deal." If we could get the whole house cleaned by 11 a.m., I would make some hamburgers and throw some Cokes in a little cooler and we would head off to Wrigley Field to watch the Cubs play. Back then, this was still possible. For me, the hour-long drive into the city and the cost of parking and tickets were worth every minute and every penny to spend that time together at the ballpark. We would watch the game and spend most of the afternoon talking and cheering for a Bull, a Rhino and a catcher named Jody (Leon Durham, Ryne Sandberg, and Jody Davis).

By the ripe old age of sixteen, it was obvious that my son lived for baseball. That summer was one of his best as far baseball was concerned. It was the summer that he was drafted by a coach who would go on to be his all-time favorite, a coach who really knew how to get the most out of my son's talent and who improved his overall game tremendously. My son was continuously working on some of the nuances that Coach Armintrout taught to him and the other boys on the team. Coach encouraged every kid on the team to work hard and achieve their absolute best. Many a night I sat on those cold steel bleachers watching, never knowing what position my son would play next, shortstop, catcher or — oh God please not — pitcher. Every time Coach Armintrout signaled for him to come to the pitcher's mound and get them out of a jam, my stomach would be in knots. Please get these guys out! Please throw strikes! Please help the team win! No matter how old your kid is, you're still his mom and you still worry. I guess I didn't need to worry that much because that was the summer he was voted team MVP.

When my son came home from college during the summer, all I had to do was throw a Neil Diamond CD in the new stereo and his ears would perk up. He knew he had better get down to business and help get the house clean. By this time, he would be the one to drive downtown and pay for parking (if I had sent him some money in the recent past), and we would walk up to the game day ticket window and spend the afternoon catching up and taking in a Cubs game.

We often talk about the amount of hours we spent watching baseball and talking in the stands of Wrigley Field. There is a special bond that my son and I share regarding the game of baseball. Baseball is a part of our family, and will always bring my son and me together no matter how old we get.

{Contributed by Jeanne Pruett}

At Fenway
[Courtesy of Dan Shaughnessy]
columnist for the Boston Globe

My first trip to Fenway Park was not the religious experience that we so often hear and read about. But it was pretty good. It was during the spring of Carl Yastrzemski's rookie year (1961), a night game against the Orioles in early June. I was in the second grade and my dad had four tickets in the upper grandstand on the first-base side. The tickets probably represented a once-a-year favor from a client in the rail freight or paper industry. My brother was allowed to invite a friend. Bill (my brother) invited Fred Porter, a fourteen-year old pal from down the street. Fred was Bill's catcher.

We went to my first Fenway game on a school night. That killed me. You knew this was important. I mean, the way my parents casually waived the bedtime curfew was enough to make a seven-year old realize this was an important event. I remember getting lost on the drive to Boston. It never failed. My father grew up on the banks of the Charles River, went to Boston College High School, and Boston College, but never seemed able to find his way around the streets of his youth. I came to expect that when we went to Boston, we got lost.

We parked in one of those lots where they take your money, then block you in for the night. We carried our jackets and bought peanuts outside the ballpark. The cheaper, sidewalk peanuts came in tightly packed brown bags. Put me anywhere on the planet, close my eyes, and hold one of those brown peanut bags up to my nose and I am seven years old, wide-eyed, gazing at the Fenway greenery. That is one the great things about Fenway and the area around Fenway. It smells like Baseball.

I had my hat and glove. We went through the Yawkey Way turnstiles and down the ramp under the third-base grandstands. The cement floor was grimy, reeked of stale beer, and was covered with cigar butts and flattened gum. Still, it was great. This was where major league ball was played, and I was walking on the same dirty ramps that the men in straw hats had walked on when they went to see the Babe. Even at the age of seven, I had the old-timey feeling. It was like being at my aunt Catherine's old house in Medford. The ballpark felt lived-in—a place where a lot of great and weird things had happened over the years. Fenway Park had been hardball home to Joe Dugan, Tris Speaker, and Babe Ruth. But we were there to see Frank Malzone, Chuck Shilling, Jim Pagliaroni, and this rookie left fielder, the great young Yastrzemski.

The best entrance to the open-air Fenway is the portal just to the right of home plate. This is an absolute. We can debate the best place to watch a sunrise on Cape Cod or the best place to see New England's leaves turn in October, but there's no room for argument when it comes to your first sight of Fenway. If you're beneath the grandstand, walk up until you come to the sign that reads, "Lower boxes 37-44, upper boxes 122-130, reserved sections 17-21."

Dad wasn't lost this time. We went up that ramp, and the majesty of Fenway's green unfolded before my very eyes. Children today probably wouldn't have the same reaction, but after years of seeing everything in black and white on our twenty-four-inch Zenith, it was the color of green that got my attention. Think of The Wizard of Oz when a young Judy Garland wanders out of her storm-shattered house and into the lush land of Oz. It's the first splash of color in the classic film, and this scene often comes to mind when baby boomer Bostonians speak of their first glimpse of the venerable Boston ballyard.

The green gets your attention. It makes the Red Sox tuxedo-white uniforms stand out. It is the backdrop that put everything into focus.

Tangled up in green for the very first time, I was struck by what seemed like the huge dimensions of the park. We always speak of Fenway today as a "small" ballpark, but when you are seven and never been far from Groton, Mass., Fenway seems very big. The left-field fence is enormous, and the lawn in right field stretches to a fence that appears quite unreachable for even the mightiest of clouters…

Finally in Fenway, I peeled some paint from a rusty rail and put it in my pocket. Maybe Ted Williams had once laid his hand on this flake of paint. It was my piece of history, something I could touch when listening to the next game while laying in bed. It was comforting and commemorative, my Fenway autograph.

Our seats for this mundane game were in the upper grandstand, under the roof, probably Section 12 between first base and right field. The Red Sox were playing the Baltimore Orioles, who had a slugging first basemen named Jim Gentile, and a rising star at third named Brooks Robinson. What did I know? Brooks looked like he was okay, but he was no Frank Malzone. Second base appeared to be the easiest position: the one with the shortest throw. Sox rookie Chuck Shilling became my favorite player. I think the Red Sox won. It didn't matter. I can't say for sure if we got lost on our way home. I was in the backseat of Dad's company car, warm with sleep, and no doubt had to be carried to my room, glove in hand, hat on head.

Bo Knows

It's the spring of 1988. I'm fifteen and my best friend, Steve, is sixteen. We are childhood chums growing up in suburban Chicago together within families that also grew up together for what seems like forever. He a die-hard Cubs fan, and I am a die-hard White Sox fan. We must have been destined to be friends, the stars lining up just so, or maybe because our families had always been close and the friendship was etched in our genes, because our baseball allegiances certainly don't explain our friendship. Spring break was on us, and we flew our chalky white bodies down to Sarasota-Bradenton Florida. Our respective grandparents had winter houses in the area, but please don't believe that seeing our families was our first priority. Baseball fever was running hot through our blood — Spring Training was in full swing. It was time for some baseball, or rather, not some baseball but as much baseball as humanly possible to consume in a week's time.

I won't go into the part about how we were able to talk with George Brett who said he'd like to meet up with us in Chicago for lunch. Somewhere in my mind I knew that was a long shot. Nor will I go into meeting one of baseball's truly nice guys, Bobby Bonilla. In fact, it's difficult to remember all of the players we met that week — the memories start to melt together into hot dogs, soda, and tickets to day and night games, warm sun on an afternoon when the snow was still falling at home in Chicago.

However, the memory that stands out most clearly is of Bo Jackson. Remember "Bo Knows"? When Bo Jackson was playing ball for the Kansas City Royals, I bought an 8 x 10 photo of him and had high hopes of getting it signed.

In person, he was truly an impressive sight. There Bo stood, just a stone's throw away at the plate. "Strike Three." The ball was clearly off the plate, no ifs ands or buts about it. Bo had a few "kind remarks" for the ump regarding his eyesight and probably a need to purchase some glasses, but he must have used one of the no-no words and this ump had his turn to shine. "You are outta' here!!" What? This is Spring training, you don't throw guys out of an exhibition game, and you certainly don't throw Bo Jackson out of a game. Is that even legal? Needless to say, Bo took the walk to the dressing rooms for an early shower. I remember thinking, "That stinks. How am I going to get my autograph?"

We started doing a little investigating around the back of the stands. Remember, this is Spring Training and these ball parks are very intimate. We found a door with a sign stating that it was off limits or restricted to park personnel – a very good sign. My friend Steve knocked on the door, and a guard opened up. We immediately looked past the guard to see a showered up Bo in a pair of blue shorts and a gray Nike cut up t-shirt. We asked the guard if we could get his autograph, and the guard rather impolitely told us to get lost. I remember seeing Bo glance towards the door and give a small smile. Little did I know what a huge heart this guy had.

By this time, it was around the 6th inning and the game was tied, and we had let every passing kid know that Bo Jackson was behind these walls. Our entourage, or perhaps an assault force that no single guard dare deny might be a better term, was forming. If Steve and I couldn't get an autograph, then maybe the collective whole of us could talk some sense into the guard and into Bo. We started a chant: "We want Bo! We want Bo!" And as kids heard the uproar and saw our group, we grew in numbers. The chant continued on louder and louder: "We want Bo! We want Bo!" And as kids can be, we had an infinite well of perseverance towards this cause—short of an army of guards with clubs, we were not going quietly. Not only were *we* going to get an autograph, but *everyone* would get an autograph. Of course, we saw this as a pipe dream in the beginning, but by the time the crowd was pulsing with the chant, we thought, "Why not? What's the worst that could happen? He says, 'No'?"

After a half hour of chanting and the crowd growing in both number and volume, the guard poked his out of the door. "Bo will sign autographs if you can get everybody to line up orderly." Well, we did it. We got those kids (and quite a large number of adults) to get in a semi-orderly line that stretched for what seemed like a mile, wrapping around and up into the stands. We did our part, and then after a couple minutes passed, Bo Jackson emerged from the door. He seemed like a giant, enormous and muscular, his chest the size of a car. Every inch of his body was ripped. "Did you two start this?" he asked because we were the first two in line. I really don't remember if I answered, but I'm sure Steve said something because he always said something. Bo signed my picture, and I still have that picture in a frame.

But the story doesn't end there. Bo Jackson not only signed an autograph for us, but he must have given one to every person at that ballpark. The game didn't end until the fourteenth inning, if I remember correctly, and he continued to sign kids' jerseys, their caps, baseballs, or any scrap of paper they could find. He probably signed autographs for well over two hours, and I want to say that it may have been as many as three. He shook hands with people, he smiled, and he made my week of baseball one of the most memorable experiences of my life.

A side note to this story: Years later, Steve and I were working for the Kane County Cougars, a single A ball team affiliated with the Florida Marlins at the time, which were in their second year of operation. Bo Jackson was in town doing a rehab assignment with the Chicago White Sox following his football injury. Steve poked his head around inside the dugout and we got to meet him again. He reminded Bo of the spring training game, and Bo immediately smiled, saying he remembered that day well.

{Contributed by Michael Cordin}

Tim Hudson
[Major League Player]

Tim Hudson was selected by the Oakland Athletics in the sixth round of the June 1997 draft. At the start of the 2003 season, Hudson had the third best career winning percentage in the history of the game behind Spud Chandler (1937-47) and Pedro Martinez. (# min. of 50 wins). He was named SEC Player of the Year his senior year at Auburn University as he excelled not only as a pitcher (15-2 record, a 2.97 ERA, and 165 strikeouts) but as an outfielder as well, with a .396 batting average, 18 HRs, and 95 RBIs. In 1999, Hudson was named the American League Rookie Pitcher of the Year by The Sporting News and finished fifth in the BBWAA Rookie of the Year balloting after his June call up. He went on to go 11-2 with a 3.23 ERA and a team leading 132 strikeouts in 21 starts for the Oakland Athletics. In his first Major League start, he struck out 11 San Diego Padres in just 5 innings of work.

The twenty-game win streak in Oakland would have to be my choice for most memorable moment. I mean, it was real exciting, especially the last five or six games because we won those games in dramatic fashion, with a couple of walk-off homers and late inning comebacks to keep the streak going. Miggy (Miguel Tejada) hit a couple of homers, and Hatteberg hit a two-run homer to win the twentieth game against Kansas City, against Grimsley. It was all so dramatic, and obviously, with a lot of media coverage there was increased pressure on the team to keep winning and keep the streak going. It was exciting! I just went out there and tried not to think about it or worry about the streak, but at the same time, you didn't want to be the guy that went out there and gave up four or five runs in the first inning to put the team in the hole so we had to try and battle back. Thankfully, that never happened. All of the games were tough, and we always battled. Even the game that we lost was a close game—it was just really exciting.

Robbie Alomar
[Former Major League Player]

After being drafted by the San Diego Padres in 1985, Roberto Alomar has gone on to have a Hall-of-Fame career and started 11 straight All-Star games from 1991 through 2001. Roberto won 10 Rawlings Gold Glove Awards, the most by a second baseman, and four Silver Slugger Awards. He owns the Major League record for consecutive errorless games (104) and consecutive errorless chances by a second baseman. Roberto Alomar had one of the most prolific decades in Major League history during the 1990s, batting .308 and playing on teams that reached the postseason six times and won two World Series. Roberto Alomar and his brother Sandy are one of four sets of brothers in Major League history to play together with three different teams.

I have a lot of great memories in this game. For example, my first at bat was against Nolan Ryan—that was an amazing experience. I used to watch him pitch when I was younger because my dad played with him on the same team, and when I made it to the big leagues, I had to face him. It wasn't an easy task, that's for sure. But going to the All-Star games and winning the World Series were great experiences and memories I will carry to my grave as well. Winning is the ultimate goal for a ballplayer.

I think people don't realize sometimes how wonderful this game is. You get to meet and play with people from different countries, and you get the chance to play with people who have a chance to go to the Hall of Fame—this is what I wanted to do all of my life. I have a lot of respect for the game, and I had the chance to play with Dave Winfield, Paul Molitor, and against Denny Eckersley… I could keep naming guys who are in the Hall of Fame right now, and I will never forget those times I had the chance to play with those guys. These are the things that I can take with me. Hopefully, I will be able to join some of my former teammates in the Hall of Fame someday.

Juan Pierre
[Major League Player]

Juan Pierre was selected by Colorado in the thirteenth round of the 1998 June first-year player draft. In 2000, Pierre made his Major League debut as a pinch runner on August 7th, and on August 8th, he beat out an infield hit, a slow roller, against Pittsburgh's Jose Silva for his first career hit. He later hit a double in that game and went 2 for 5 for the day. Pierre continued to hit the ball remarkably well, starting his Major League career with a sixteen game hitting streak in which he hit at an impressive .359 clip for its duration. His is considered one of the longest streaks to start a career in Major League history. In the 2003 season, Pierre became the first Marlin to record 200 hits in a season, and he led the Major Leagues with 65 stolen bases. That same season, he received the James "Cool Papa" Bell award from the Negro Leagues Baseball Museum. In 2004, Pierre led the National League with 221 hits and 12 triples. In four of the five seasons between 2001 and 2005, Pierre was the single most difficult player to strike out in the National League. In addition, he has played in every game in the 2003, 2004 and 2005 seasons.

Definitely for me the most memorable moment is winning the World Series in Yankee Stadium. I saw a highlight clip of me running in from centerfield, probably running as fast as I could. As I was running in, I remember having thoughts about playing T-Ball, little league, high school and college baseball. When I was running in to be with my teammates, it was like I could see my whole career go flashing in front of me because that is what you always dream about growing up, winning the World Series. I don't know how many times while I was playing in my backyard that the bases were loaded with two outs, and to actually have it happen to win the World Series has to be one of the best feelings I have ever had in my life.

Where Would You Like to Eat Tonight?

My husband Chuck and I had the opportunity to have dinner at Red and Mary Schoendienst's house. In case some of you are unfamiliar with the great Red Schoendienst, he is one of the most beloved Cardinals of all time, a ten-time National League All-Star and Hall-of-Famer on and off the field.

Red happens to be the uncle of a lady in our parish, and our kids all went to school together. The woman in our parish managed to get Red to offer a dinner at his house as an auction item, and my husband and I bought an entry and won a place at this party.

Just being in their home and having cocktails and dinner with them was exciting enough, but at one point, I turned around and in walked Stan Musial and his wife Lil. My husband and I almost fainted! After dinner we were all sitting around and Mary Schoendienst, who had a wonderful voice, sang for us and Stan jumped up, whipped out his harmonica and played for us too. After that, dessert was served. I looked around for a place to sit, and there was Stan Musial, all by himself. Do you think I hesitated? I walked up and asked if I could join him. I then proceeded to spend the next thirty minutes chatting with one of the greatest baseball players of all time. One of the greatest experiences of my life!

{Contributed by Sandy Sullivan}

Rich Aurilia
[Major League Player]

After earning All-Big East honors at St. John's University, Aurilia was selected by the Texas Rangers in the twenty-forth round of the June 1992 draft. He won the 2002 John Hancock Roberto Clemente Award for his tireless work in the community, that same year he showed his phenomenal ability with the leather as well, as he led all National League shortstops in Fielding Percentage with a .980 mark. In 2001, Aurilia had a remarkable season at the plate, joining some prestigious company in Willie Mays and Bobby Bonds as the only other San Francisco Giants to have over 200 hits in a season with 206. He also became only the third shortstop in National League history to hit 30 home runs in a season.

I was on deck, ready to hit next in the 2002 National League Championship Series when we scored the winning run to go to the World Series. So I was the first guy to greet David Bell at home plate and celebrate with my teammates. It was extra special being at home in San Francisco. The crowd was so loud it felt like the ground was shaking. It's what you play for your whole life. When you're a kid that's what you want to do—go to the World Series —and it was great to be right there and experience it first hand. I've witnessed Barry Bonds hit about 400 home runs and steal about 350 bases as his teammate, so I am fortunate in that sense too. When I am done playing, I can say I was teammates with the best player ever.

Pokey Reese
[Major League Player]

*I*t *was only a matter of time until Pokey made his presence felt in the big leagues The two-time recipient of the Rawlings Gold Glove winner (at second base) was rated by* Baseball America *as the best defensive player in the 1991 Major League First Year Player Draft. He recorded his first hit in the Major Leagues off the Florida Marlins' Rick Helling on April 12th 1997 as a member of the Cincinnati Reds. It was a two-out single in the bottom of the tenth inning to score Eric Owens with the decisive run in the 2 to 1 contest.*

My most memorable experience was winning the championship in the Arizona Fall League on a team called the Mesa Saguaros. Bruce Kimm was managing us. We had the youngest team out there, and nobody really had any expectations for our team. We had guys like Brant Brown, Cory Lidle, and Aaron Boone—we had a lot of good guys on the team. There was a guy named Antoine Williams who was a real good player. Even though he didn't make it, he was a first round pick for the Milwaukee Brewers. I think what made us special was the team chemistry. We won our first eight games, and no one expected that. We simply gelled as a team and put everything together. Bruce Kimm told us to go out there and don't worry about the game, to be relaxed out there and have fun. He said, "Even though we may not have the best team, we're going to go out there and play hard everyday."

Barry Zito
[Major League Player]

Barry Zito, the ninth overall player in the June 1999 draft, found immediate success in the Major Leagues by winning the 2002 American League Cy Young Award. At twenty-four years of age, he was the youngest player since Roger Clemens won the Cy Young in 1986, who was also twenty-four when he first won the prestigious award. Zito was also named the 2002 American League Pitcher of the Year by Sporting News. As a junior at USC, Barry was a first team All-America selection by USA Today Baseball Weekly, Collegiate Baseball, and Baseball America as he went 12 and 3 with a 3.28 ERA and 154 strikeouts in 113.2 innings.

When I was at USC, I had three games in a row that stick out. I struck out 16, then 16 and another 14 guys in three successive games, and that was cool to be able do that. Another memorable moment for me was during my rookie year, when I beat the Yankees in the 2000 Playoff elimination game in 2000. We were down 2 to 1, and we had to get the Series back to Oakland. We scored 11 runs and were able to beat Clemens, so that was pretty cool.

Note from the author: During the summer between my junior and senior year at USC, I had an internship in northern California and went with a couple of people to the Oakland A's–Anaheim Angels game. It was a beautiful late July northern California day, and obviously, I was excited to see Barry Zito pitch his first big league game. He looked incredibly poised and it reminded me of how he used to pitch when he was still at USC and playing for the Trojans, dominating the rest of the Pac-Ten Conference. But this was different—,this was the Major Leagues. To this day, when I think of Barry Zito, the moment that really stands out for me is from this game.

After loading the bases in the fifth, he proceeded to strike out the next three batters in succession to get out of the inning unscathed and with his first Major League win. The batters that Zito faced to get out of the fifth were no bush leaguers either, but the heart of the Angels lineup: Mo Vaughn, Tim Salmon and Garret Anderson! The roar of the home crowd was enough to give even the most casual of fans goose bumps! So, when I asked him about that moment as well, he paused ever so briefly as if to play it back instantaneously in his mind's eye and then flashed me a million dollar grin and said, "Oh Yeah! That is another one of those that really sticks out too. That was pretty awesome!"

Shawn Green
[Major League Player]

G reen was selected by the Toronto Blue Jays with the sixteenth pick in the first round of the 1991 first-year player draft. In 1994, he recorded his first Major League hit on June 13*th* off of Cleveland Indians pitcher Mark Clark. In the following year, his first full rookie season, Green led the club with a .509 slugging percentage, the highest mark by a Blue Jays rookie. In 1998, he started to find his groove and became the first player in Blue Jays' history, and just the ninth player in the American League history, to collect thirty homeruns and thirty stolen bases in the same season. In 2001, after being traded to the Los Angeles Dodgers before the 2000 season, Green became the fifth person in Major League Baseball history to hit forty or more homeruns in both leagues, having hit forty-two with Toronto in 1999.

My most memorable moment came in a game in Miller Park in Milwaukee (May 23, 2002),when I had six hits and four homeruns. *Shawn was six for six with four long homeruns, a double, a single and six runs scored, and he drove in seven RBIs and set a Major League single-game record with nineteen total bases.* It is something I was very fortunate to have happen to me. I think for something like that to happen all of the stars have to be aligned the right way. I enjoyed that day, and I'll always remember it. I saw the ball really clearly, and I was real relaxed and confident. It was like that for me the whole week. I hit three more homeruns in the next two games, and I finished the week with a total of nine homeruns, but that game was special and I knew it.

Kenny Lofton
[Major League Player]

While at the University of Arizona, Lofton was the starting point guard for the Wildcats and played alongside teammates Steve Kerr and Sean Elliot. Lofton was selected by the Houston Astros in the seventeenth round of the June 1988 free-agent draft. In 1992, after being traded to Cleveland, he finished second in American League Rookie of the Year honors (behind Milwaukee's Pat Listach) and broke John Cangelosi's record of 50 stolen bases for a rookie with 66 swipes. Lofton followed up these numbers during his sophomore campaign with 70 stolen bases while batting .325 and scoring 116 runs. The six-time All-Star and member of the Cleveland Indians All-Century team played in two consecutive National League Championship Series under Dusty Baker, with San Francisco in 2002 and the Chicago Cubs in 2003. In 2004, he played in his sixth League Championship Series, this time as a member of the New York Yankees.

In 1995, when I was still with Cleveland, we clinched the division against the Seattle Mariners and then played in the World Series. Cleveland hadn't been to the World Series, in man, I don't know how long, and it was just great! When we got that last out, everyone was so excited and we all jumped around the field and we were all shouting, 'We're going to the World Series!' We had a great group of guys and had a lot of fun in the clubhouse, and we took that good time we had with each other out onto the field and won. That has been my most memorable moment in the game so far.

Sandy Alomar Jr.
[Major League Player]

Alomar originally signed with the San Diego Padres as an amateur free agent in October of 1983, and he was traded to Cleveland in 1989 along with a couple of additional players for Joe Carter. In 1990, he joined Carlton Fisk (1972) and Mark McGwire (1986) as the third player to be unanimously chosen as the American League Rookie of the Year by the BBWAA (Baseball Writers Association of America). He became the first rookie catcher in Major League history to start in the All-Star game, and over the course of his career, Alomar played in six All-Star games and two World Series (1995 and 1997).

There are always a lot of memorable experiences in baseball, and one of the most exciting ones was getting my first Major League start in San Diego. I was so nervous and excited that I couldn't stop sweating, even when I was just walking around before the game. My first hit was off of Tim Cruz of Cleveland. I hit a double to left. It was a great experience. *After talking with Sandy awhile, I asked him what it was like to play with his younger brother, Robbie Alomar. This is what he had to say*: We grew up playing together in the little leagues and then in the Minor Leagues. For a couple of years, we played separately, and he was in a lower level since he signed later. But it was such a great experience to grow up playing with your brother and to watch him develop his skills and mature as a player over the years.

Josh Beckett
[Major League Player]

Beckett was the second pick overall in the first-round of the first-year *player draft by the Florida Marlins in 1999. By 2001, he was the Marlins' top minor league prospect and the number-three prospect overall named by* Baseball America. *He made his Major League debut against the Chicago Cubs on September 4, 2001, allowing one hit and striking out five in six innings in the Marlins' eight to one win. In 2003, Josh became the youngest World Series MVP since twenty-two year old Livan Hernandez won it with the Marlins in 1997, six years earlier. In 2005, he set new career bests in wins (15), complete games (2), innings pitched (178.2) and strikeouts (166).*

I would have to say winning the World Series in 2003 has to be the most memorable moment I have had so far, especially now that I have had some time to look back on it. There isn't any way to actually describe what it was like being there and pitching at Yankee Stadium, but you definitely feel like you are on top of the world there when you win a World Series.

Beckett became the first pitcher since Minnesota's Jack Morris in 1991 to pitch a complete game shutout in a deciding World Series game, and just the nineteenth overall in baseball history. He became the youngest pitcher to win a deciding World Series game since Kansas City's Bret Saberhagen in 1985. Beckett struck out forty-seven batters in the 2003 postseason, tying Randy Johnson (2001) for the all-time record for a single postseason. It's something even as a kid I dreamt about. Pretty much every kid has played in the seventh game of the World Series in their backyard, and the count is three balls and two strikes. Instead of getting that hit to win it, I got to throw the pitch and live out every kid's fantasy.

John Smoltz
[Major League Player]

Smoltz was drafted by the Detroit Tigers in the 22nd round of the 1985 June amateur draft, which is considered the greatest draft in Major League history. The draft included Barry Bonds, Randy Johnson, Will Clark, Mark Grace, Mark McGwire, and Barry Larkin. After being traded to the Atlanta Braves for Doyle Alexander in 1987, Smoltz made his Major League debut on July 23rd of 1988 against the New York Mets, going eight innings and giving up only four hits and one earned run. The seven-time All-Star has played in the midsummer classic in three different decades: the 80s, 90s, and 00s. He won the 1996 National League Cy Young Award after leading the Major Leagues with 24 wins. In 2002, Smoltz won the Rolaids Relief Award as the best closer in the National League with 55 saves. From 2002 through 2004, John averaged 48 saves a season. In 2005, he returned to his original starter role and won 14 games with an ERA of 3.06. John joins only Hall of Fame inductee Dennis Eckersley as the only pitcher with over 150 wins and 150 saves.

The ride in 1991 has to be the most memorable for me. Not only pitching the seventh game for the pennant and then pitching the seventh game of the World Series; it was truly a dream come true. It was borderline euphoria, having a chance to win two of those types of games in a career, let alone in one year. Unfortunately we came so close, and I pitched the way I wanted to pitch, but ultimately we didn't come up the end result that we wanted. Probably the most memorable situation for anyone who has played this game would be pitching in a seventh game of the World Series.

Growing up, I always envisioned doing that as a kid, and you never know how it's going to play out, and what the game would be like, ultimately it fulfilled every dream I could have imagined.

When I asked John, what was it about the clubhouse that made this organization so successful, this is what he had to say. It would have to point back to Bobby Cox, our manager. What he brings everyday with his consistency and it carries throughout our clubhouse and it shows up on the field. It has just been great to be around him everyday.

J.D. Drew
[Major League Player]

After his junior season at Florida State, J.D. Drew was named the Player of the Year by Baseball America *and* The Sporting News *and received the 1997 Golden Spikes Award and the Dick Howser Award after hitting .472 along with 28 homeruns and 94 RBIs. While at FSU, he became the first player in NCAA history to hit 30 homeruns and record 30 stolen bases in a single season. He signed with the St. Louis Cardinals a year after being drafted by the Philadelphia Phillies, and he went on to make his Major League debut the same game that Mark McGwire broke Roger Maris's single season homerun record. In his fourth big league at bat, he collected his first hit, a 438-foot homerun off of lefty Gabe White in Cincinnati.*

Playing in the College World Series was incredibly memorable—it's a fun environment with half the crowd rooting for one team and the other half of the stadium rooting for the other. College baseball fans get really fired up about the games, but playing in the big leagues and playing in different stadiums on the road with the way home stadiums root for their team is pretty crazy too.

But I think getting the chance to watch Mark McGwire break the single season homerun record with number sixty-two and then go onto to hit number seventy is up there on my list of memorable moments too. The situation was pretty chaotic, and I think he really handled it well and did some special things for the game. He got people fired up about the homerun chase again and made it fun to watch.

Mike Hampton
[Major League Player]

After a great high school career and ultimately turning down offers to play football at Florida State and the University of Florida, Hampton signed with the Seattle Mariners, who drafted him in the sixth round of the 1990 June draft. In 1999, after being traded to Houston in 1993, Hampton had a career high for wins in a season (22) and finished second in the Cy Young voting behind Randy Johnson. In 2002, while with Colorado, he earned his fourth Silver Slugger Award, leading all Major League pitchers with a .344 batting average. In Atlanta in 2003, Hampton became the first pitcher to ever win a Rawlings Gold Glove and Louisville Silver Slugger award in the same season.

Probably the most memorable moment for me was the National League Championship Series in 2000, when I was pitching for the New York Mets. I pitched the first game of that series and the last game as well. I threw a complete game shutout to clinch the NLCS and help the team get to the World Series. *In the 2000 National League Championship Series, Hampton was nearly perfect in the two games he pitched against the St. Louis Cardinals. In sixteen innings, he struck out twelve and didn't give up a run.* My focus was there from the first pitch to the last pitch. I really had my mind set on winning, and my concentration was absolutely dialed in for that game and that series. My confidence was at an all-time high, and everything was just rolling in the right direction. It was one of those rare games that I had everything working. It seemed like Mike Piazza couldn't put down a wrong signal, and whatever he put down, I felt like I could throw it, so it was a lot of fun. It was one of those games that was just really fun to participate in, when you know all your stuff is working and you can throw any pitch at any time.

Mike Lowell
[Major League Player]

*L*owell was selected by the New York Yankees in the twentieth round *of* the 1995 June Free Agent Draft. In 1998, Lowell made his *Major League debut against the Toronto Blue Jays' Kelvim Escobar and collected his first big league hit in his first at bat. In February of 1999, Lowell was traded to the Florida Marlins, and shortly thereafter, became Randy Johnson's 3,000th strikeout victim on September 10, 2000. Lowell represented the Florida Marlins in the 2002, 2003 and 2004 seasons as a member of the National League All-Star squad. In 2003, he also received the Silver Slugger Award, which is presented to the best offensive players in each league.*

My most memorable moment was definitely during the playoff run in 2003. Personally, it was the at bat in which I pinch-hit in Game 1 of the NLCS in Wrigley Field. My hand was broken in interleague play and I still wasn't 100%. I hadn't played in September at all, and I had only played in one game in the series before with the San Francisco Giants. I was still having a few weak at bats, so thank God there was a three-day layoff between the end of one series and the start of the next. With the rest, I started to feel a lot stronger, even though it was a cold October in Chicago.

It was late in the first game of the NLCS, and in fact, I was leading off the eleventh inning. I remember thinking that I just wanted to hit the ball hard and try to get the inning going. I was fortunate to have a big hit, and my homerun put us up by a run —we went on to win the game by one run so it definitely worked out great. As for a memorable moment from a team standpoint, just feeling the total satisfaction of winning the World Series has to be the high point. Having the chance to experience the game from that perspective is the best moment and highest achievement you can have as a ball player.

Andruw Jones
[Major League Player]

*O*riginally drafted by the Atlanta Braves in the 1993 amateur draft, Jones made his big league debut just three years later in 1996. In the 1996 World Series, Jones became the first National League player (and second overall) to hit two homeruns in his first two World Series plate appearances. At 19 years old, he passed Mickey Mantle to become the youngest player to homer in World Series history. He has continued to build from his early success, winning eight consecutive Gold Gloves and playing in four All-Star Games. In 2005, Jones finished the season leading in two of the three Triple Crown categories: homeruns (51) and RBIs (128). He also led the entire Major Leagues in homeruns and was the only player to hit over 50 for the year.*

Everyday something happens and everyday, it is special. This is a special game, and everyday we go out there and try to learn something new and get better. Whenever I put on my uniform before a game, it's great. I love this game so much, and even when I am struggling, I still put the uniform on the same way I do when I am doing well. I love to play this game, and everyday I am here, it's a great feeling.

Reggie Sanders
[Major League Player]

Reggie Sanders was selected by the Cincinnati Reds in the 7th Round of the 1987 free agent draft. He is one of only six players to hit 20-or-more homers with five different Major League teams joining Bobby Bonds, Jose Canseco, Jack Clark, Fred McGriff and Dave Winfield. In the past six seasons dating between 2000 and 2005, Reggie has played in the post season five of the six seasons, including appearances in the 2001, 2002, and 2004 World Series. The first being with the World Series Champion Arizona Diamondbacks and in 2002 he helped lead the National League Champion San Francisco Giants to their first pennant in thirteen seasons. Reggie was an integral part of the St. Louis Cardinals' run to face the Boston Red Sox in the 2004 World Series. Most recently, in the 2005 National League Divisional Series, while batting .385 against the San Diego Padres, he set the Major League record (in only three games) for most RBI's with 10 passing Carlos Beltran's previous mark of 9.

What stands out the most in my mind is getting that first opportunity to come to the Major Leagues. I was playing AA ball in Knoxville, TN at the time when it happened. I got a call from Bob Quinn, who was the General Manager of the Cincinnati Reds then, and he said that it was time for me to come to the big leagues. I was like 'Who?!' Bob paused and said, 'YOU... We'll have a plane ride set up for you to come up tomorrow, and Reggie, we're excited to have you."

Of course the Cincinnati Reds were excited to have him. Not only was Reggie hitting .315 with 8 homers and 49 RBIs, but they were getting a speedy outfielder who was leading the Southern League with 8 triples at the time of Bob Quinn's call.

Getting that opportunity to step out on the field for the first time, and back then it was Astroturf in Riverfront Stadium, was awesome! I remember the first ball that eventually was hit out to me in the outfield. I couldn't wait for the fly ball to come down, so as it was still descending, I literally jumped up to catch it. I was that excited!

Eric Munson
[Major League Player]

*A*fter finishing his career at the University of Southern California
and ranking third in the nation in home runs (44), fifth in slugging
*percentage (.655), seventh in batting average (.356), and ninth in RBIs
(147), Eric Munson was the Detroit Tiger's top pick (third overall) in the
June 1999 draft. He was the NCAA East Regional Most Valuable Player
and a finalist for USA Baseball's 1999 Golden Spikes Award as he helped
lead USC's World Series Championship run. Munson collected his first Major
League hit on September 19, 2001 off Eric Milton at Minnesota, and a
couple of weeks later hit his first Major League home run, again off of
Milton, on October 3rd.*

I think winning the College World Series was my most
memorable baseball moment. That is the biggest thing I have been
a part of as far as winning. Obviously, being in the big leagues is
a lot of fun, and that is the ultimate goal you work for, but my
favorite memories are from winning it all in 1998.

It was a lot of fun. The whole town shuts down and everybody
comes to watch you play, and when you have a Tuesday afternoon
game and there are 25,000 people there, it gets real intense. The
players all want to win it, and they're throwing their bodies all over
the place. It was amazing!

David McCarty
[Major League Player]

McCarty *was* Baseball America's *College Player of the Year in 1991 and earned both first-team All-American and Pac-10 Southern Division Player of the Year honors. In his sophomore season at Stanford, McCarty hit .336 and helped pace the Cardinal to a third-place finish in the College World Series. He signed with the Minnesota Twins as the third overall pick in the first round of the 1991 June first-year player draft.*

There are three memorable experiences that really stand out for me. The first one was a couple of years ago, in 2003, when we made it to the playoffs. It was just an incredible experience. The atmosphere was like nothing I had ever experienced from a team standpoint.

My most memorable individual moment was hitting a walk-off homerun in Boston in 2004. I hit the homer in extra innings off of J.J. Putz, a reliever for Seattle.

The third moment that really stands out occurred earlier in my career, which was in the latter part of Nolan Ryan's career. I grew up in Houston, and I used to go watch him when he was with the Astros. Ryan is kind of a hero of mine. I was with the Minnesota Twins at the time, and we were playing the Texas Rangers. It was Nolan Ryan Day at the ballpark, and I think it might have been his last home start of his career there. It was a big situation too. There were two outs late in the game, and I fouled a few pitches off and then hit a double. To knock him out of the game on his day was pretty special for me, and to be able to have an at bat like that against one of my boyhood heroes was just incredible.

Dontrelle Willis
[Major League Player]

Willis was selected by the Chicago Cubs in the eighth round of the first-year player draft. Willis was later traded to the Florida Marlins in what is now one of the most talked about trades in Chicago Cubs' history. In 2003, he was named the National League Rookie of the Year and was also the winner of the Larry Doby Award, which is given out by the Negro League Baseball Museum for National League Rookie of the Year, after he set the Marlins' single-season record for wins by a rookie and finished tied for the team lead with 14 victories. In 2005, he was named to National League All-Star team for the second time and continued to build on his success by leading the National League in wins (22), complete games (7), and shutouts (5).

All the experiences that I have had in baseball have been memorable: taking all those bus rides, traveling through Vancouver, Canada and then getting promoted to AA and being able to see the whole Southern League and going through all those little cities and then getting the call up to Major Leagues. I went from riding the bus to all of a sudden taking charter flights to our own little airports — and it's just the whole experience. Going through years of that and then making it, but having to work so hard to get here makes you really appreciate it and everything that comes your way. It is definitely a blessing going through all that. Not only is baseball the best game in the world, but once you make it to the big leagues, you definitely want to stay here.

Chapter 3

Calling the Shots:
Coaches and the Front Office

Rick Cerrone
[Director of Media Relations, New York Yankees]

Even though I have been here for a relatively short period of time, there have been so many memorable moments being a part of the New York Yankees. Since I have been here, I have seen two perfect games and a pitcher throw a no-hitter. These were all quite memorable. Away from the game, I would have to say the most memorable experience for me was going down to the area near the World Trade Towers shortly after they were attacked and still smoldering. We, by that I mean the Yankees organization, went down to the Armory to sit with the families as they were gathering to await word on their loved ones. We visited the staging areas to offer help and support.

To know these ballplayers that fans gather to see at ballparks on a personal and professional level is something special. I get the opportunity to know what kind of people they really are and to see firsthand all of the extraordinary things they do in the surrounding communities. When I see, for example, the way Derek Jeter responds to a sick child or takes the time to sponsor kids in a program, all while handling everything that he is given to deal with, is really an amazing thing. That goes for everybody on the whole team.

Although we didn't win the World Series following the tragedy of September 11, that post season was quite memorable. Getting through that 2001 playoff series with Oakland was quite a challenge. We were down 2 games to 0 before we knew it, but with Yankee resolve, the team found a way to come back and beat Oakland.

What stood out in that playoff series was the amazing presence of mind in a play made by Derek Jeter. It happened right in front of me. It probably should have been a bang-bang play at the plate, but anything can happen in the playoffs. I was standing in the tunnel between the dugout and the clubhouse, and I remember thinking as Shane Spencer's throw overthrew the cutoff man, 'That ball is not going to beat him to the plate.' Then out of nowhere, Jeter rushes in and flips the ball blindly behind his back to Posada who makes a sweeping tag to punch out Jeremy Giambi at home. Not many people could have made that play.

Then during Game 3 of the 2001 World Series, which was at Yankee Stadium, with President George W. Bush on hand to throw out the first pitch...Wow, the stirring that night. Despite your political views, to be able to watch the President of the United States take the walk out to that fabled mound and have the composure to throw a strike the way he did in that atmosphere was breathtaking. American flags were waving proudly in that crisp New York autumn air, and people were cheering themselves hoarse — some could barely see beyond the tears welling up in their eyes.

The next two nights were just as dramatic with Scott Brosius' tie-breaking RBI to win Game 3 and then Tino Martinez's two-run home run in the bottom of the ninth to tie the game and Derek Jeter's walk off home run in the tenth to win Game 4. One home run like that was unbelievable, but to see two sensational home runs like that? We started to think that it was almost as if something greater was at work there. But despite eventually losing the Series to the Arizona Diamondbacks, there were quite a few memorable moments that postseason.

Frank McCourt
[Owner, Los Angeles Dodgers]

When I sat down to talk baseball with Frank McCourt, the owner of the Los Angeles Dodgers, a couple of things really stood out for me during our conversation: how important his family is to him, both past and present, and his unbridled passion for the game of baseball...

From my vantage point, being in a strong family and bringing family ownership back to the Dodgers has become sort of a metaphor for the larger Dodger family. It just so happened that the Dodgers were on the market and we were freshly off an effort to buy the Boston Red Sox, but knock on wood, everything has worked out wonderfully. In my case, my grandfather was a minority owner of the Boston Braves and it (ownership) was in my blood a little bit — it wasn't something that was completely foreign to me.

I think it makes a big difference when you have a family ownership or family stewardship, it's just different than a corporate situation. There are faces, there are real people... I cheer with the fans, and I get upset with fans at the same time they're upset. We sort of laugh and cry together, and that is where the passion reveals itself. That's where the emotional bond between ownership and the fans, and of course the players, is so important. The Dodgers have had a very wide reach, whether it is breaking the color barrier or the move west from the east coast, that has really changed the country. These are the things that go beyond baseball. It is part of our history, our culture, our past.

Baseball is the greatest sport, it's about competition, it's about winning and losing, but it also is about a lot more than that. It's about handing the game down from family member to family member from generation to generation. These are things that I think make baseball truly our national pastime. I think there are a number of things that allow baseball to be passed on generationally with such ease. I think it is that way for a number of reasons. There is nothing like when you are a kid and you pick up a glove and go outside and play a game of catch, oftentimes with your dad. When you get a little better at the game, you're off to the ball field to play pick-up games with neighbors, siblings, and friends. It doesn't matter where you play it, in the driveways, in the backyards — you just play baseball anywhere, making up rules for what qualifies as a single, what qualifies as a double or homerun while you probably listen to the game being called on the radio. It is part of growing up.

Another part of it is the social aspect. Unique to baseball versus the other sports, you can ask someone, "Do you remember the first professional baseball game you went to?" Almost all the time, the person that you are talking with will remember that first game exactly. If you ask who they were with, they could tell you most all of the time exactly who they went to their first game with. Oftentimes, it is Dad, Mom and Dad, or Granddad, a family member or a family friend. If you ask if they remember who won or lost, they seldom will remember that. I don't think that, if you ask somebody the same question about the first time they attended other professional sporting events, they will necessarily have the same vivid memory of that first outing. I'm not trying to take anything away from these other sports, but it's just the impression that was left is stronger for baseball because of the importance of the game to our culture, the way it is so deeply woven into this culture. There is something majestic walking into that ballpark for the very first time. It creates an indelible impression, and there is something about the game that is so hopeful.

The way the game is played with the concept of starting at home and striving to get back home, the ebb and flow of the games, the ebb and flow of the season. You can sit and have a conversation with somebody and watch a game or listen to a game. If you are listening, you can immediately know that something has changed by just the sound of the game. I think it is more difficult to have the same social interaction while watching other sports because there is a different rhythm to the game. There is a different aspect to it.

Baseball starts up in the spring and you get caught up with it in the summer and your hopes are either dashed or rewarded in the fall and it starts all over again after resting for the winter, like a natural thing. I think there is something about the game engrained in who we are at an early age too, because it is engrained in our culture. I tell people who come to work for us from different countries or cultures, if you want to get to know America, go to baseball games. Learn about baseball, and you'll learn about our culture.

Most people partake in it as a player or as a spectator or participant in some broad way, and we all have these good memories, and at the end of the day, we all are striving to find time — time to spend with our family and our friends. That is ultimately our most precious commodity and we are all in constant search of it. What is really wonderful about a baseball game is the time it allows you and how it is spent: three captured hours you have to just enjoy it, being in sort of your home away from home with people who are either your guests or of whom you are guests by choice, often family and friends. And you are part of a broader community with that in common. That is a pretty unique thing. We all really cherish that type of time well-spent.

It is everyman's sport still. It really does have an aspect to it, a quality to it, because many people played it. When they were little, they picked up that ball, hit it, threw it, and ran the bases, played the games and had the experiences. The game is not something that is foreign to almost anyone. It is something that is very familiar to them and brings back a lot of great memories. Therefore, they're knowledgeable about the game, and so there is that notion that people like a player because 'he plays the game the way I would play the game if I could be out there.' There is that kind of identity, and they can live vicariously through their favorite teams' and players' experiences. It is a way for people to have opinions, and strong one's at times, about their favorite player and what should be done in a given situation and what was done right, what was done wrong, a coach's move, a GM's move, what the manager should have done or should not have done, what a particular player would have done in a given situation… There is a lot going on in a baseball game, and so there is a lot to relate to. On the other hand, you don't need to know a lot about baseball to enjoy the game, because it is easy to get the big picture. You go, you watch it, you love it and have fun.

My first game, I went to Fenway. I was with some siblings and family… It was sort of family day at Fenway. It was just a fantastic experience. I can remember sitting there yelling and cheering, and just being able to cheer on my hometown team. I can't tell you who won or lost, but I remember where I was sitting. I remember who I was with, the smells, the sounds, the sights, the feeling… It is still very, very vivid. Every game transports you back to that moment — it is what all that was built on. Then you build a lifetime of memories, and God willing, new memories are created as the baton is passed. That is why my favorite thing over the years is spending time with my kids at the ballpark. That was sort of my duty in a way, to pass on the love of the game. When I see people coming here to Dodger Stadium and I hear it is their first visit, it really perks up my attention because I want to make sure that visit is a great one! Then I know they'll be involved for life.

I don't care to admit how many hours I have spent in ballparks over the years, far too many, but then again, not nearly enough. I can remember being at one game with my youngest son and we were sitting in a box at Fenway Park. It was towards the end of the game, and the Sox were playing the dreaded Yankees and there was a foul ball hit in our direction. There were a couple of boys sitting three rows ahead of us, and they all had brought their gloves. They saw the ball coming, and they reached their fullest to catch the foul ball. The older brother had a little longer reach, and he got his glove just on the ball, but not enough, and the ball deflected off his glove. The ball hit a column and ricocheted off a wall and landed right at my feet. So after a little scuffle for the ball, I grabbed it, and I turned to my son, who was either six or seven at the time, and handed him the ball. It was the first time I had gotten a foul ball. After all the times I had been to the ballpark, it was the first time, but I handed it to him and I could see the wide-eyed excitement in him. He was already a huge fan, and when I gave him the ball, he sort of looked at it, and then I saw a very slight change in his facial expression. It caught my attention. He sort of looked at me, and then he looked away. Then he walked down the stairs and walked to the younger boy who had missed the foul ball a minute earlier and gave the ball to him. It was such a great moment between a father and his kid. To see your kid do that. The boy who received the ball was even more wide-eyed than my son because he got that baseball, the one that he almost had moments before. The game was over shortly thereafter, and I just put my arm around my kid and we walked out of the ballpark.

Speaking of memorable baseballs: a couple of years ago (2004) in spring training, at my first game as the steward of the Dodgers, we were sitting right behind our bench. There is no dugout there in Dodgertown, just the bench for the players and coaches. I remember I was sitting right behind Jim Tracy, the manager, and Hideo Nomo went out to the mound and threw the first pitch to start the game. The umpire, by the name of Bruce Froemming, was behind the plate. He's a *real* pro and has been doing this for years and years. After Nomo threw the pitch, you could hear the POP of the catcher's glove. Bruce Froemming, in a big burly voice, yells, 'Striiiike!' The batter just stood there, even though this thing was grooved right down the middle of the plate. With that, Froemming stands up and takes his mask off, and he turns and looks over right at Jim Tracy and says something. I couldn't tell what was said, and I was wondering what was happening. I was thinking this is spring training and there has been only one pitch. What's going on between these guys and is this some sort of carryover from last season? Froemming started walking right at Jim Tracy. All this took place in a matter of seconds, and as he was coming toward the bench, I kept thinking, 'What is going on here?' Then I realized he wasn't walking over to our manager. He was walking over to me, and my first reaction was, 'What did I do?' and I stood up and was leaning against the railing. I mean, he had stopped the whole game. He puts out this big paw and shakes my hand and says, 'Mr. McCourt, welcome to the big leagues.' And he took the ball that Nomo had thrown and the catcher had handed to him, and reached out and handed it to me. When I looked down at the ball, I saw that, as an incredible gesture, he had the entire umpire crew that day, sign the ball. He was aware that it was my first game as an owner and knew how much it meant to me, and he handed me that ball with all the signatures on it. We have become great friends since, and it was such a wonderful moment for me. In many ways, when we win that next championship for the Dodgers, that ball to record the last out will be incredibly important, but the one Bruce gave me will remain so special for me.

Kevin Towers
[General Manager, San Diego Padres]

K evin Towers has been involved in professional baseball either as a player, scout or executive for over twenty-three years. After a successful pitching career at Brigham Young University, the San Diego Padres selected Towers in the first round of the 1982 First-Year Player Draft. After spending two years as a scout with the Pittsburgh Pirates, he returned to the Padres organization in 1993 as the new Director of Scouting. He became the team's General Manager in November of 1995 and was named Executive Vice President/General Manager in March of 2000.

Well, for me it would have to be playing the Yankees at Yankee Stadium in the 1998 World Series. I was a young General Manager, and I think it was my third year with the San Diego Padres. I took the number four train to the stadium with manager Bruce Bochy, and it was especially memorable for us because we had coached together in the Northwest League in Spokane ten years earlier. It was almost like, 'Wow, look at where we are at now!'

Walking out to centerfield and going through Monument Park, past busts of Babe Ruth, Lou Gehrig and Mickey Mantle, really added to the historical feel of Yankee Stadium. All of that was memorable, but the opportunity to watch the team that you're responsible for putting together playing for a chance to win a championship was incredible. Just remembering watching as the ground crew spray painted the Padres logo on the field right in front of the dugout as we were warming up for the first game in the World Series still gives me chills to this day. That 1998 Yankee team is arguably one of the best teams of all time, and we were playing them in the World Series at Yankee Stadium. We were four and out, but we played them very well, and a couple of games could have gone either way.

Plus, the excitement in the playoffs leading up to the series, like the Randy Johnson-Kevin Brown match up in Game 1 of the National League Divisional Series, when Kevin shutout the Astros for eight innings and struck out sixteen batters and allowed only two hits to earn the win. Ultimately, we beat the Houston Astros in four games and then beat the Atlanta Braves in the National League Championship Series to get back to the World Series for the first time since 1984.

Prior to coming to San Diego to work with the Padres, I used to be a scout in the Pittsburgh Pirates organization. The memory of watching Atlanta Braves pinch hitter Francisco Cabrera knock us out in Game 7 of the 1992 National League Championship Series is still vivid in my mind. *Francisco Cabrera's 9th inning, two-out, two-run, pinch-hit single drove the winning runs in to beat Pittsburgh 3 to 2 and send Atlanta to the World Series for the second consecutive season.*

Cabrera's hit cost me a chance at getting a championship ring and going to the World Series in 1992, so to be able to knock the Atlanta Braves out six years later, especially being a GM rather than a scout, was pretty rewarding. So I would have to say those memories are the ones that stand out most so far.

Ellis Burks
[Special Assistant, Cleveland Indians]

B*urks was drafted by the Boston Red Sox as the twentieth player chosen in the first round of the 1983 January free-agent draft. In 1987, Burks had an exceptional rookie season, hitting .272 with 94 runs scored, 30 doubles, 20 homers, 59 RBIs and 27 stolen bases. He became the first Red Sox rookie and third player overall to hit 20 homers and steal 20 bases in the same season. In 1990, he was named to the American League All-Star team as an outfielder and went on to win a Rawlings Gold Glove and Silver Slugger Award. In 1996, Burks had his best overall offensive season and was named to his second All-Star team with the Colorado Rockies, hitting .344 and setting a career high in homeruns with 40. He also had 128 RBIs and finished third in the National League Most Valuable Player voting. In 2002, while with the Cleveland Indians, he was named baseball's top designated hitter after hitting .301 with 32 homers and 92 RBI in 138 games.*

My most memorable moment would be my first game in the big leagues. To even get to play at this level is an opportunity that few players are blessed to experience, and so that first game is one that stands out for most Major Leaguers. I got the opportunity in 1987.

I was with the AAA Pawtucket Red Sox, and it was a funny thing, but we had the day off (April 30, 1987) and I was out renting some movies. Our General Manager left a note on the door of my apartment while I was out, asking me to call him as soon as I could and saying that he had some good news and some bad news for me. As soon as he picked up the phone, I asked him to give me the bad news first, but he didn't. He said the good news was that I had been called up to Boston, but the bad news was that the team was up in Seattle and they wanted me on the six o'clock flight. I looked at my watch, and it was about 3:30 at the time!

Obviously, I made it to the game in Seattle, but the experience was pretty nerve wracking. I didn't know what to pack, and so I started just throwing stuff in my suitcase — and I just made it to the airport in time! I was so excited that, while I packed, I was calling everyone I knew, and they were excited for me too and congratulating me. It was a lot of fun. Scott Bankhead was pitching in my first game, and I went 0 for 2 with a strikeout and grounded back to the pitcher. I even dropped a ball in the outfield, a low line drive that fell out of my glove.

Paul Mainieri
[Head Coach, University of Notre Dame]

My greatest experience in baseball had to be the day Notre Dame defeated the consensus #1 team in the country, Florida State University, to clinch a spot in the 2002 College World Series. The significance of what we achieved in itself would have made it the most memorable moment of my life in baseball, but some extenuating circumstances added to its significance in my personal life.

The night before the final game of the NCAA Super Regional (both teams had won one game each in the best of three series), my wife (who was there with me in Tallahassee) got word that her father had been put in a hospice house in Toledo, Ohio and no one knew how much longer he was going to live. I spent the evening before the biggest game of my life trying to get her and my children out of Tallahassee and back to Toledo so that she could be with her father before he passed away. Fortunately, a Notre Dame booster, Frank Eck, flew her back to Ohio and she was able to spend the last few days of her father's life with him. My wife, Karen, insisted I stay with the team and coach in the game the next day.

When I went to the field the next day for the final game of the series, I was filled with mixed emotions. I was excited about this situation our team was in because I had a wonderful group of kids who had been with me for up to four great years, and I wanted very badly for them to achieve this unbelievable accomplishment. Yet, at the same time, I couldn't help but wish I was with Karen and her father because that's what a good husband is supposed to do—support his wife at times like these. I understood completely that there were things that were more important than baseball.

When we were in the ninth inning of that game and holding on to a 3 to 1 lead, three outs from accomplishing what most people thought was impossible, I couldn't help but think of my wife and what she was going through. When our great relief pitcher, J.P. Gagne struck out the side in the bottom of the ninth to send us to Omaha, the myriad of emotions running through my mind was almost too much to handle. I was so happy for the kids in our program and what this accomplishment meant to all those who had worn the Irish uniform before them. I had reached the pinnacle of my profession as a college baseball coach, taking a team to the College World Series in Omaha, but I didn't have my wife and children there to share the moment with me – and that made me feel very empty.

My father-in-law died on Friday of the next week, the day before we were to open the College World Series against Stanford. He was buried on Monday, which was also my wife's birthday and the day we beat the *new* number one ranked team in the country, Rice University. We beat Rice with a three-run rally in the bottom of the ninth inning, which was capped off by a home run by Brian Stavisky. My wife, who was watching the game with her mother on ESPN back in Toledo, told me later that night it was her father who blew the ball that Stavisky had hit out of the ballpark.

Jeff Pentland
[Major League Hitting Instructor]

A fter pitching at Arizona State University for three years and playing in the Minor Leagues, Jeff Pentland came back to his alma mater and became the ASU hitting coach in 1983. This is where he began working and developing future Major Leaguers Mike Devereaux, Mike Kelly, Oddibe McDowell, Fernando Vina and Barry Bonds. In 1992, Jeff joined the Florida Marlins scouting staff and in 1996 he was elevated to the Major League Hitting Instructor for the second half of the season. In 1998, he went to work for the Chicago Cubs as their Major League Hitting Instructor working with Sammy Sosa, Mark Grace, Fred McGriff, and newly inducted Hall of Famer Ryne Sandberg. He worked with the Kansas City Royals as their Major League Hitting Instructor from the 2002 through the 2004 season.

Barry Bonds was such a great athlete when I had him at Arizona State as a developing, young player. His power numbers weren't what they are now, but he had power, there is no question about it. I think the most memorable thing about Barry for me was the first time I ever saw him when I was hired at ASU and he was hitting on the field. I walked over to the field and watched him as he hit eleven straight balls over the scoreboard in straight away center, which was something I had never seen before, and I said to myself, "Wow, this guy could be something special." I certainly didn't realize how special he was going to be, but Barry was very young and even then, had a great feel and instinct for the game. Having a dad like Bobby and being around his Godfather Willie Mays, he obviously grew up around baseball, and he probably had the greatest instincts for the game out of anyone I have ever seen. Even when he was young, he could see pitches earlier than anyone. When I had him, his swing wasn't as pure as it is now, but I remember very distinctly that I would challenge him with particular pitchers.

We had a game against Stanford, for example, and Jack McDowell was pitching. I thought Jack was the best college pitcher I ever saw, and I remember that I challenged Barry, telling him this guy was so good he was going to strike him out three times. I think Barry responded with two home runs against him. He was so good in college that sometimes I think he was a little bit bored with some of the teams we played against, but when we went up against some of the great pitchers and out to Omaha, he was always very, very good.

I also had Gary Sheffield in Florida, and at that particular time, I had never seen a right-handed hitter quite as good as Sheff. I remember him hitting a home run off both Ugeth Urbina and Pedro Martinez in the same day. He just hit them a ton right down the line, and the radar guns had the pitches coming in at 98 or 99 mph. In fact, Urbina tipped his cap to him after he hit that one off of him. Sheff was a different person in his ability to get up for a game and a different person in his love for hitting. I never met anyone who loved hitting more than Gary Sheffield. I think the greatest moment for me with Gary was one time when he was frustrated and he said, 'Jeff, I don't think I am gonna get another hit...,' and I just told him to stay in there and hit the ball back off the guy's forehead. The pitcher he faced was the other Martinez back in LA, and the guy had a really good arm. I think Gary missed his head by about an inch, and when he came back in the dugout he said, "I think I got it."

Kelly A. McCord
[Message Therapist, San Diego Padres]

I had the unique opportunity to meet with Kelly McCord, who is the first-fulltime female massage therapist in the Major Leagues and is equally kind and engaging as she is talented in her profession. In order to be the first anything, you have to overcome great odds and certain stigmas. After spending a few minutes with Kelly, the phrase, "those who said it can't be done are getting passed by those who can" entered my mind and stayed there long after our conversation ended. When I asked her how she got started working with professional athletes, this is what she had to say:

When I was still in massage therapy school, I happened to get paired up with a customer who had requested a student studying sports massage. I was due to graduate in a couple of weeks and to take my medical board exam, so the school paired me up with this client. He liked his massage so much that he asked if he could have a business card and refer me to some of his friends who were professional baseball players. I gave him my card and let him know that I was graduating and would be available for regular clients after I took the State Board exam. I really did not think for a minute that one of the Cleveland Indians players would call me, but they did.

There was a day in November of 1995 that Carlos Baerga called and asked if I was available to work with him that afternoon. He explained that his normal therapist was busy and could not fit him in, and that he received my card from his friend who had come to the school to get a massage. Of course, I was excited to work with him, and he liked his massage and the sports therapy so much that he invited me to attend spring training to work with him and other players from the team. I did attend Spring Training in 1996, and to my surprise, I ended up working with about 70% of the team!

After Spring Training, the players that I was working with kept me busy during the season and invited me to Spring Training again the following year.

As you know, players get traded all the time. In 1997, Alan Embry and Kenny Lofton were traded to the Atlanta Braves from the Cleveland Indians. That Spring Training they asked me if I would drive to Orlando to continue to work on them, and in return, they would get players from their new team to make the trip to Orlando worthwhile for me. I made the 45 minute-drive from Winterhaven, FL and started working with a lot of the Atlanta Braves players. One of those players was Ryan Klesko. He liked the treatment so much that he asked if I could travel during the season to continue working with him. When Ryan got traded to the San Diego Padres, he told me that he wanted me to come with him. He told me that he would take care of talking to the trainers to see if I could work out of the training room and that he would take care of all of my travel expenses. I continued to travel with Ryan, and the head trainer for the Padres, Todd Hutcheson, agreed to allow me to work out of the training room even though the team was not paying me. This was a huge accomplishment, since prior to this I was only working on players outside the ballpark. I continued working in the training room during spring training and on selected road trips from 2000 to 2003.

At the end of the 2003 season, Todd Hutchinson told me the Padres were looking to hire a full-time massage therapist for the upcoming season and asked if I would be interested. I made sure that he and the front office personnel knew I was very interested, but at the same time, I knew it would be difficult for an organization to take that "leap" and hire a female. So, needless to say, when Todd called me in late October and said they had made a decision to hire someone, that he knew I had gone above and beyond in every aspect when I was working with the players, I was waiting for the 'BUT, we have decided on someone else.' Instead I heard the words, 'I would be proud to have you on my staff.' Those words and the feeling that I had at that moment will never leave me and will always be by far the most memorable moment of my career. I finally did it. I finally was able to break those barriers and show the world that it doesn't matter if you are a male or female, that what matters is, finding the best person for the job.

That year was filled with many memorable moments: posing with Ryan Klesko, Trevor Hoffman and David Wells for *USA Today's Sports Weekly*; the numerous articles that were written; the interviews; the TV shows like *This Week in Baseball*. But none of that was more significant to me than walking out on the first-base line for the ceremonies on Opening Day, first at Dodger Stadium and then at our home ballpark Petco Park.

I did achieve one of my dreams, and I hope I have touched someone's life as much as mine was touched the day I heard the words that will never leave my heart: "I would be proud to have you on my staff."

Richard "Itch" Jones
[Former Head Coach, University of Illinois]

After returning from a good freshman year back in 1993, one of my young players, Josh Klimek, went through fall baseball and improved tremendously. One evening in November, near the completion of fall baseball, he was involved in an accident with an automobile on his moped. I was at a speaking engagement in Toledo, Ohio when I received a call from my assistant coach, Dan Hartleb, that Josh was involved in the accident.

That Monday I saw Josh in the hospital, and he had broken his leg and injured his shoulder. The doctors set the leg with four rods running from the foot to below the knee. Several weeks later, Josh's leg was removed from the cast and the doctors informed us there was a good chance that Josh would never be able to sprint again. Josh started physical therapy and worked hard to recover.

During the 1994 season, which he missed, he sat next to me at a number of our home games, and we discussed the game of baseball.

Thirteen months later, in January 1995, Josh was still rehabbing but he had a bad limp. Again I confronted the doctors and they gave me the same story. By March, his limp was gone and he was beginning to work out with the team in our indoor workouts.

In the 1995 season, he made a stunning comeback, leading the Illini with a .361 batting average. He was named first-team All-Big Ten at shortstop. He hit .382 with a team-leading .647 slugging percentage in nineteen Big Ten Conference games. Josh handled 72 chances at shortstop without an error in league games and helped turn twenty-six double plays in forty-four games. He missed twelve games with a dislocated shoulder after sliding into second base in a March game against Purdue. Not bad, since this was the same guy who couldn't walk without a limp. Josh enjoyed hitting streaks of eleven games, seven, five and four games, while making just 9 errors in 195 chances, which is a .954 fielding percentage. Josh was our anchor on the best fielding University of Illinois team in school history, with a team .971 fielding percentage.

In 1996, following a great 1995 season, Josh Klimek lead the NCAA Division I in home runs with twenty-six, and he became a First Team All-American/All Big-Ten, and Big Ten Player of the Year.

Josh graduated from University of Illinois and played professional baseball as high as AAA. He is an amazing person who had a great college career.

Barry Larkin
[Special Assistant, Washington Nationals]

B*arry was destined to be a member of his hometown Cincinnati Reds after being drafted by them twice, the first time in the 1982 free agent draft after he graduated from high school and the second time in the 1985 draft after attending the University of Michigan. He was the fourth player selected in the 1985 draft and played nineteen seasons with the Cincinnati Reds. The twelve-time All-Star went on to win nine Silver Slugger Awards, three Gold Gloves, and was awarded the 1993 Roberto Clemente Award, the 1994 Lou Gehrig Award, and the 1995 National League Most Valuable Player Award. In 1996, he became the first shortstop in Major League history to record more than 30 homeruns (33) and 30 stolen bases (36) in the same season. During the 1990 World Series, he paced his team with a .353 batting average and helped them sweep the Oakland A's in four straight games.*

The most memorable experience for me was back in 1990, when we won the World Series. It is a team sport and everything seemed to click for us as a team. Personally, I had a good year, but it just seemed like everything we did or tried to do went well. There were a lot of games that we probably didn't have a reason to win or shouldn't have won, but we somehow found a way to win. Lou Pinella was in his first year with us in Cincinnati as the manager, and everything he did seemed to click for us.

We had a real fiery clubhouse, and there were a couple of fights, even the highly celebrated case between Rob Dibble and Lou Pinella, but I think that is what we needed at the time. Lou really brought over that fire and intensity and the club just responded to it. It was a memorable season for sure.

John Schuerholz
[General Manager, Atlanta Braves]

A native of Baltimore, Schuerholz left a job as junior high school teacher to join the Orioles in 1966. He moved on to Kansas City a couple of years later and was involved in the expansion draft that created the inaugural Kansas City Royals roster. During his time with Kansas City, the Royals won one World Championship, two American League pennants (1980 and 1985) and six division titles (1976, 1977, 1978, 1980, 1984, and 1985). In October of 1990, Schuerholz joined the Atlanta Braves as GM and started building towards one of the greatest professional sports records of all time, assembling Atlanta Braves teams that have won fourteen consecutive divisional titles. When the Braves won the 1995 World Series, Schuerholz achieved a rare feat when he became the first General Manager of a Major League team to win a World Championship in both the American and National Leagues. At the time of this printing, Schuerholz has been associated with three World Championships (1966 with Baltimore and 1985 and 1995 with Atlanta) eight pennant wins, and twenty division titles.

I would have to say winning my first World Championship as General Manager really stands out. Being actively involved in the creation of a roster that goes on and wins the World Championship, as I was in 1985 in Kansas City, is really special.

In terms of team wins, my most memorable season was 1991, which was my first year in Atlanta. Expectations for the team were low, and people were even sort of laughing at us and our franchise, but we ended up going to the World Series and almost winning it. We went up against a great team in Minnesota, and they won it in Game 7. Now that was a great match-up—Jack Morris and

John Smoltz—and it was one of the best games ever played in a World Series.

But winning the first World Championship for the city and community of Atlanta in 1995 was probably the very best baseball moment imaginable. That was the first time in the history of baseball that a General Manager had won a World Championship in both the American and National Leagues.

I didn't know that until a public relations person told me, and I am proud of that accomplishment.

One of those wonderful moments for me was also watching George Brett get inducted into the Hall of Fame. I met George when he was seventeen years old. He reported to Billings, Montana as a Carl Yastrzemski-like hitter who played shortstop, and he eventually became an All-Star and Hall of Fame third baseman. We have always maintained a great relationship over our professional careers, and we still have a great friendship. I was delighted to see him get that supreme honor and was delighted to see his success all along the way.

On the sad side of most memorable moments, I had the misfortune of watching a friend of mine, Dick Howser, die of a brain tumor while he was managing our team in Kansas City. That will stick with me all my life.

Overall, there are just too many people to mention that I have had memorable moments and conversations with over the years in baseball, but some important ones still jump out I suppose. For example, the streak of fourteen consecutive titles has been a thrill too. I don't want to take anything for granted and we are doing something that no other team in any sport has done in history. In this day and age, with so much roster fluidity and roster changes because of a variety of circumstances, being able to win fourteen consecutive division titles is a great accomplishment and a real tribute to this organization.

Tony Muser
[Major League Coach]

F ormer manager of the Kansas City Royals, Tony Musser finished
   third on the all-time Royals managerial win list behind Whitey
Herzog and Dick Howser. He spent nine seasons in the big leagues as a player
with four different teams: the Boston Red Sox, Chicago White Sox, Baltimore
Orioles, and the Milwaukee Brewers.

I have been involved in professional baseball for over thirty-six
years. I think that my most memorable moment was playing in my
first game in the big leagues. I was with the Boston Red Sox and
played my first game in Yankee Stadium on a Sunday afternoon.

On that particular Sunday afternoon, they had a mini bat give
away so the stadium was jam packed. It was a great ballgame, and
I got my first Major League hit off of Mel Stottlemeyer, who had
started the All-Star game earlier in the year, and my first Major
League RBI. It was the thrill of a lifetime. I remember that I was
so excited when I got to first base that my feet went numb and
I couldn't feel them.We ended up losing that game 2 to 1. Dick
Williams was managing for us at the time, and Ralph Houk was the
manager of the Yankees in 1969.

But when you're involved with the game for a long time, there
are so many great memories to choose from. I got to play with
Brooks Robinson in Baltimore, and Mark Belanger the shortstop,
Paul Blair, Boog Powell, Lee May, Jim Palmer…just great teammates
and a lot of great memories.

But I think everybody's first game in the big leagues is always
a great memory. As the manager of the Kansas City Royals, I had
the opportunity to watch about twelve guys get their first big league

hit. There was a relationship there between the memory of my first hit and knowing the thrill the twelve guys felt getting there first Major League hit. I knew how important it was for them, and it is fun to watch a young man work hard his whole life and make it as a professional baseball player.

Mike Gillespie
[Head Coach, University of Southern California]

Having been involved in baseball for some time, I have a couple of memorable moments that stand out most for me. We won the national championship in 1998, and certainly winning in itself was extraordinarily memorable, but more memorable for me than simply winning the national championship was the performance of our players during that week at the College World Series. I mean this in terms of "hit and runs," getting timely base hits. We had players execute the squeeze, drag bunts, push bunts for base hits, and we were six of seven in stolen bases, including stealing home. We asked our players to hit behind the runners and move them over to second base with no one out. We had five guys who responded with doubles, and not just hitting it to the right side but hitting doubles to the right side gap! Again for me, more memorable than winning was the extraordinary effort and performance of our players for the duration of the tournament.

We actually lost the opening game to LSU and had to come back in the double elimination tournament of the College World Series. In fact, we beat LSU later in the week. We had Seth Etherton on the mound for that game, who was the *Sporting News* Player of the Year and a consensus All-American. Later on in the tournament, we depended on a freshman named Rik Currier against Mississippi State in an elimination game, and he struck out twelve batters in a remarkable performance. Mike Penny pitched well for us also, as did Jack Krawczyk, who was an All-American and set the single season record for saves that year. After beating LSU twice, we had to play Florida in the championship game, and that game went into extra innings. We were in the tenth inning and the score was tied at 8. They had runners on first and second, and the hitter due up next was Brad Wilkerson. We chose to walk him intentionally, which consequently put the winning run at third and forced us to face the right-hand hitting, number four hitter in the lineup, Casey Smith. Smith already had two hits and four RBIs in the game. The count went to three and two against Smith, and Krawczyk threw a perfect three and two changeup that induced a little groundball back to the mound. Krawczyk threw it over to first and we won the championship!

I think the other single most memorable period of time was the extraordinary performance of Mark Prior in the 2001 season. Mark Prior has become a household name in the game of baseball, and only injury could keep him from being all that people expect of him at this point. For me, he is at the head of the shortest list of premier and elite pitchers in the game. I genuinely think he can prove to be one of the great pitchers in the history of baseball.

In his Junior season with us, he was 15 and 1, and ultimately he was named the Player of the Year by every organization and major publication — he made a clean sweep of it. He was the first player to ever have done that. Since, Jared Weaver has won all of these awards too, but with Mark, it was the first time anyone had done that before. In 2001, he threw 138 innings, struck out 202, and walked 18 — two of which were intentional so he really walked 16. He'll never forgive me for walking the two guys intentionally because he was sure he could've gotten them out.

Actually, his one loss that year was 2 to 0 to Stanford. Both runs were unearned — and we failed to score for him that day. His consistency from pitch to pitch, inning to inning, game to game was just bizarre. His pitching was really almost mystical, it was so consistent. When you combine that with the quality of person that he is, in terms of personality, unselfishness, work ethic, demeanor, loyalty—he becomes the single most memorable individual player for me as a coach.

Bobby Cox
[Manager, Atlanta Braves]

Cox is recognized as one of the greatest baseball managers in the history of the Major Leagues. He has guided the Atlanta Braves to fourteen consecutive division titles, which is phenomenal even when compared to other historic sports dynasties: the great Boston Celtics won nine consecutive division titles and the Colorado Avalanche also won nine consecutive division titles. The only team that has a claim of being a more successful dynasty than the Bobby Cox led Atlanta Braves would be the New York Yankees teams from 1947-1964, when they won 15 of 18 divisional titles (including 10 World Series Championships) but never more than 5 divisional titles in a row.

The one moment that I remember vividly is my first ballgame as a Major Leaguer in 1968. As I stood there at third base in Yankee Stadium listening to them sing the National Anthem, I got goose bumps. Just being at Yankee Stadium and looking around and seeing Mickey Mantle had me awestruck a bit. It was an experience that I have never forgotten, but the truth is, just showing up to the ballpark everyday is the greatest thing that could happen to a guy.

Chris Chambliss
[Major League Hitting Instructor]

*C*hambliss *was originally drafted by the Cincinnati Reds in 1967 and again in 1969, but he elected to play in college. He eventually signed with the Cleveland Indians after being the first pick in the January 1970 free-agent draft. In 1971, after hitting .275 in 111 games, Chambliss went on to win the American League Rookie of the Year with the Indians.*

After being traded to the New York Yankees in 1974, Chambliss was voted to the American League All-Star team in 1976 and won a Gold Glove at first base in 1978. In the 1976 American League Championship Series, Chambliss hit .524 while breaking or tying five League Championship Series records for hits and RBIs.

That is pretty easy. It was back in '76. It was really a fun year because we went into the newly refurbished Yankee Stadium and played a great season. I think we won the division by about ten games, and then played the Kansas City Royals in the playoffs and had a real battle with them. Back then it was the best-of-five to put you in the World Series. The ALCS (American League Championship Series) was tied at two apiece, and in that next game, we had gone ahead and they tied it up in the ninth inning. That's when I hit a homerun to put the Yankees in the World Series. *Chambliss hit a monster bomb off the first pitch he saw from Kansas City's Mark Littell in the bottom of the ninth inning to take the New York Yankees back to the Fall Classic for the first time since 1964.*

George Horton
[Head Coach, Cal State Fullerton]

It is hard to separate out the memories that I am most fond of, but you tend to remember your first kiss, your first date, the first time you played catch with your mom or dad, the first time meeting a college ballplayer or pro ballplayer. I suppose all of my firsts in baseball would qualify as the most memorable, but I have been in baseball for over thirty years and have been so spoiled because there have been so many positive things that involve the game in my life. I remember my first championship as a player very fondly, and I remember my first championship as a coach at several different levels.

The 2003 NCAA baseball championship meant so much because of who we were competing against — the University of Texas. Not only because of what that school's baseball program means to college baseball because of their tradition and the quality of their team, but one of my mentors, Augie Garrido was the coach of that team. You would have to go a long way to get any more special than that as far as winning is concerned.

I didn't know it at the time, but the environment that I was blessed to grow up in has a lot to do with what I am doing today. I have vivid recollections of being a bat boy for college-age kids in a park when I was eight or nine years old. The interaction and learning environment that was presented to me as a youngster as I watched how they carried themselves and heard what they would say was priceless, and I remember paying attention to those role models and wanting to be like them. They would pay me fifty cents a game for chasing foul balls, money I'd use for candy at the snack bar later in the day.

I participated in baseball in high school, but I got passionate about baseball when I learned about it from Wally Kincaid at Cerritos College. That is when it became a sport that gave you examples for life, and it became a sport that I saw myself coaching. I learned the X's and O's and the philosophical basis of success, and I also learned the mentality a player and a coach needs to face the challenges that baseball brings to all of us. It is a failure sport. It is a sport that will knock you on your rear end if you let it.

That is what I think about most often when I think about baseball — the necessary mental aspect of baseball that is so important and how difficult it is to grasp. The whole experience is more about the game to me now. It is about life. It is about relationships. It is seeing these guys succeed off the field. And the bar got raised awfully high with the group of kids we had who won the National Championship, because they were the best group I have ever been a part of. For them to be rewarded with a National Championship is pretty special, and I don't know if we could do that again. We could win a National Championship, but to have a group with those types of personalities involved would be remarkable.

Baseball... It is all of the days that I spend with the players and coaches, the David Snows, the Augie Garridos, and playing for the Kincaids who have all become like family, and to be in those environments in which I was able to learn. Early on, I thought it was about teaching the sport of baseball, but now I realize it is more about the sport teaching the human being. We are teaching the players how to do *things* right, not just baseball right. That way, the human being always wins.

Tim Wallach
[Major League Coach]

Wallach led the Cal State Fullerton Titans to the College World Series title in 1979. He also picked up the Golden Spikes Award (top amateur player in America) and was the named The Sporting News College Player of the Year. *Wallach, the five-time All-Star third baseman and three time Gold Glove winner, is the all-time leader for Montreal Expos in games, at-bats, hits, doubles and RBI.*

When I came up (to join the Montreal Expos), one of the great things was that the whole club really treated me well. So I would have to say my favorite memory of baseball is probably the way they treated me. I respected them, but because they treated me so well they taught me the way to treat other guys who were coming up as well. Even though we got beat in the National League Championship Series in 1981 and never made it to the World Series, just getting to play with those guys is a great memory. Guys like Andre Dawson, Gary Carter, Steve Rodgers, and Larry Parrish and a lot of other guys really had a huge influence on my career, and that is something I'll always remember.

Lance Parrish
[Major League Coach]

*L**ance Parrish, the eight-time Major League All-Star, was the first pick (16ᵗʰ overall) for the Detroit Tigers in the June 1974 draft. He won the Silver Slugger Award at catcher six times, won three Gold Gloves, and ranks among the best Major League catchers of all-time with a .991 career fielding percentage. Parrish ranks seventh in Major League history for total games caught with 1,818 and also ranks in a tie for fourth among catchers with 324 career home runs and is ninth all-time with 1,070 RBI's.*

It would be easy for me to say winning the World Championship in 1984 with the Tigers was the most memorable moment. Obviously, that is a huge highlight in my career, but I think just getting my first opportunity to put on a big league uniform and to know that I was on a Major League team is what really stands out for me.

It was a dream come true to finally make it to the big leagues when I was called up in September of 1977. Just knowing that I was going to have an opportunity to play was probably the biggest thrill in my life.

In my first game, we played the Baltimore Orioles, and I went 0 for 2. The next day, I got my first big league hit off Earl Stevens and went 3 for 4. In that game, I not only got my first hit but my first double and my first home run! It was a really big night, especially since my folks were able to be there in the stands to see it and share those moments with me.

Tony Peña
[Major League Coach]

P eña was originally signed as a non-drafted free agent by the Pittsburgh Pirates on July 22, 1975. In his eighteen year career, he caught in 1,445 games which is fourth all-time behind Carlton Fisk (2,226), Bob Boone (2,225) and Gary Carter (2,056) while winning four Rawlings Gold Gloves and voted to the National League All-Star team five times.

In 2003, Peña was selected as the American League Manager of the Year by the Baseball Writers' Association of America after leading the Kansas City Royals in his first season as a Major League Manager.

I have to say that the most memorable experience for me was when I came to the United States as an eighteen year-old boy and had to learn a new culture in a new country. That included some real tough lessons in my life too. However, in my career, one of the best memories I have, is when I was able to put on a big league uniform for the first time. I am never going to forget being around Willie Stargell, Dave Parker, and Chuck Tanner, the manager. I will never forget about all those great moments we had and the great players around me who made me a better player. Those veterans played with the type of intensity that was inspiring, players like Phil Garner, Manny Sanguiellen, Omar Moreno, and Bill Madlock. When those people took the field, they did so with one thing in mind: to go out there and be successful by playing the game the right way. I grew up learning to go out there and do whatever it would take to win the ballgame, and now in my coaching career, I try to pass that along to some of the young players. I try to take what I learned from the great players and show the young guys how to play the right way. I always believed that, if you are around great people and you are a great person, you too will become great.

Pat Murphy
[Head Coach, Arizona State University]
Former Head Coach, University of Notre Dame (1988-1994)

With the encouragement of my father, I became fascinated with Notre Dame athletics while growing up. To be named the head baseball coach at Notre Dame in August of 1987 was a dream come true for this 27-year-old from Syracuse, NY. While my seven years in South Bend provided several priceless memories, one of my favorite Notre Dame baseball moments came during the 1989 Midwestern Collegiate Conference tournament.

As is still the case today, the winner of a conference tournament receives an automatic bid to the NCAA tournament. We won the conference regular season and entered play as the top seed. We won our first game but were then upset by the University of Detroit in the second game, which meant we would have to go through the loser's bracket and win five straight games in order to win the tournament. To complicate matters, the weather was brutal and there were significant rain delays. The forecast for the rest of the tournament was also less than encouraging, so tournament officials decided that games would continue through the night. In essence, to pull off the tournament win, we would have to win these *five games in under 24 hours!*

Instead of looking at it as five games and a seemingly impossible mission, we decided to break down the task ahead into 45 innings. If we could either tie or win every inning, we would win the conference crown and advance to the NCAA tournament. To help us track each inning, Pat Eilers, one of our outfielders and also a football player, flattened one of those boxes that the new baseballs come in and wrote a chart detailing 45 innings. For every inning we won or tied, he stuck his finger in the mud around the dugout and put his fingerprint on the chart under the respective inning number. As we got deeper into the tournament, there was a huge rally cry around this "mud chart," as it became called, almost like a "win one for the Gipper" type of thing.

As it ended up, we won five games in just under 23 hours, with one of those games starting at around 2 a.m. We would send various players home in the middle of the night to rest, but our catcher, Ed Lund, wound up catching all five games! Mike Rooney, former Arizona State assistant coach, and current Major Leaguer Craig Counsell, also played all five games. One of our pitchers, Joe Binkiewicz, closed game four and turned back around to start game five of the "The Odyssey." It was a situation where everyone had to contribute and did. By winning the automatic bid, Notre Dame received our first NCAA tournament bid since 1970.

Our program was only blessed with four scholarships, and yet we finished the season 48 and 19 and ranked in the Top 25 for the first time in decades. Our tournament win was even big enough news for *Sports Illustrated* to mention it in the "Scorecard" section. Given the circumstances surrounding this accomplishment, it was a moment I am still very proud of, and every time I talk with a player from the 1989 Notre Dame team, we recount this unbelievable feat.

Ozzie Guillen
[Manager, Chicago White Sox]

*G*uillen *was drafted by the San Diego Padres as a free agent in December of 1980. He was traded to the Chicago White Sox and was named the American League Rookie of the Year in 1985. Guillen was a three-time American League All-Star during his twelve seasons with the White Sox. He later played with Baltimore, Atlanta and Tampa Bay. He retired with the second highest career fielding percentage (.974) amongst Venezuelan shortstops, behind Omar Vizquel and in front of Dave Concepcion, Luis Aparicio, and the legendary Chico Carrasquel. Guillen is the first native of Venezuela to manage a Major League team and is the sixteenth former White Sox player to also manage the club.*

After so many years in my baseball career, it is hard to pick one moment that stands out alone, but there is nothing like being in the World Series. *Guillen was in the World Series as a player with the Atlanta Braves in 1999 and as the third base coach with the Florida Marlins in 2003, and then as Manager of the White Sox in 2005.* I was in the World Series three times, and winning two championships was the most amazing thing I have ever been a part of in my career. Winning the American League Rookie of the Year was special for me, but always my dream was to win a Gold Glove and I did it. I loved watching guys like Luis Aparichio, Vizquel, and Concepcion —all of us coming from Venezuela—and that is still one of my favorite awards and one of the best experiences I have ever had in the game of baseball.

Bob Todd
[Head Coach, Ohio State University]

I've been very fortunate in my life. I've had many, many positive and fulfilling experiences as an athlete. I was a three-sport athlete in high school, and so sports certainly occupied my time. There is no question that my love for baseball was paramount, however.

Growing up in St. Louis, which I consider the best baseball city in America, there were always little leagues, summer ball, and American Legion teams. Those rosters were always full—there were just many, many kids playing the game of baseball in my town. As we know, baseball is a game that includes failure more than any other team sport, and that can make the game very frustrating. Consequently, when I was growing up, the person who had the biggest influence on my attitude about the sport of baseball was my dad. He told me to stay on an even keel mentally. He taught me to enjoy everything I do and to always do it to the best of my ability. Maintaining a positive attitude was important. Winning and losing was secondary.

One of the more memorable baseball experiences of my life happened during my senior year of high school. We had a very talented and experienced team, and in fact, we started the year ranked number one in the state and with everybody predicting we would win the state championship. I was fortunate enough to be elected captain of this team. But we lost three of our first five games. These teams were not nearly as well coached or talented as we were. Fortunately, we righted the ship and won a league championship, a district championship, and regional championship, and made it to the finals of the state championship, going undefeated the rest of that year.

In the semifinal game of the state tournament, our power-hitting first baseman was in a collision play at first base, severely hyper-extending his elbow. Some people thought he may have even slightly dislocated it. The next day, when we were set to play for the state championship, he couldn't straighten his arm out, but he was bound and determined to be in our starting lineup. Doctors gave him permission, and they taped up his elbow where it was literally at a ninety-degree angle. From the first inning on, as you can imagine, every infield ground ball requiring a throw to first caused huge anticipation as to how good the throw was going to be or whether he was ever going to be able to get his glove to the baseball to make a catch.

We were fortunate and jumped out to an early lead. As the game progressed and our first baseman had to handle the baseball often, there were some anxious moments. I think it goes to show you that some things just happen for a reason, but as the tension mounted, it seemed like every throw that an infielder made was always in the middle of the first baseman's chest so that he barely had to move his arm. As luck would have it, we didn't make any errors and we won the State Championship. Overcoming that adversity, and constantly hearing my dad's voice in the back of my mind, reminded me that "God never gives you a challenge that you can't handle."

Raymond "Smoke" Caval
[Head Coach, LSU]

Obviously, most people would think the National Championships of 1991 and 1993 would be the memories that stick out the most, since those were our first two here at LSU and we worked so hard to get there. We had such a great bunch of guys who worked so hard and were very talented, but one of the funny things is that the next question that was asked of us immediately was, 'Can you do it again next year?'

But there was a weekend series that we had down in Texas back in 1989 that really stands out in my mind. Back in 1989, we were in a six-team regional tournament, and LSU wasn't as solidified a program as we are now. We knew that going over there to College Station, Texas (home of the Texas A&M Aggies) was quite a tough challenge for us since their fans were known to be really vocal. I think they were like 58 and 7, and even though we had one of the premier pitchers in the country, Ben McDonald, a Golden Spikes Award winner, we didn't swing the bats all that well yet. It wasn't "gorilla ball" like it is now. In fact, I think we hit under .300 as a team with about 60 homers. It wasn't like we were going to blow teams out, but we did have a team ERA of 3.60 in 72 games. So we sent our ace, Ben McDonald, out against UNLV, and he only made it through the first three innings and gave up six runs — it wasn't looking real good. They had Donavan Osborn throwing lefty, and he was bringing it pretty good. But that humidity sure played a factor and caught up with those kids from Vegas, and before you knew it, we had come back to take the lead 9 to 6. Eventually, we won the marathon, but we ended up using a lot of our pitchers.

It was such a great environment in College Station, but a tough place to play. In our second game, we faced off against South Alabama. They ended up beating us 6 to 4, and again we used four more pitchers, and the fans down near Texas A&M were equivalent to verbal Freddy Kruegers. They kept coming after us and continued to hammer us.

After losing to South Alabama, we dropped into the losers' bracket. We had to try to sneak a win in there, and our pitching staff was so thin that we went with a freshman, Chad Ojay. Chad later went on to pitch in the big leagues with Cleveland and might have been the MVP of the 1997 World Series had they won the whole thing, since he had a couple of wins and even got a couple of hits. Had I known that he could hit that well, I might have let him swing when we had him at LSU. He gave us eight strong innings, and we beat UNLV for the second time. After the win, we went back up into the winner's bracket and played against South Alabama again, but this time we beat them 6 to 5.

Now, to win this whole regional tournament, we had to go up against a Texas A&M team that had only lost seven games all season. Not only that, but I don't think they had lost one game at home all year. So our chances weren't looking all that good, but the one good thing we did have going for us was that we had Ben McDonald available since he had only pitched for three innings in the first game against UNLV and was ready to go for us. Like I mentioned earlier, those A&M fans were ready for us. They had the bags from McDonalds with the Golden Arches across the front of them, and they had holes cut out for their eyes and had them covering their heads. It was pretty neat, actually, a pretty cool sight. I mean these fans really created a great atmosphere. And we had to beat these guys *twice* to get through the regional and on to Omaha for the College World Series. Yes, we had McDonald going for us, but if we won, we didn't have any idea who we were going to have pitch next.

So I decided, even after we saw that they had the field all set up for pre-game batting practice, not to take it that afternoon. It was way too hot and our pitchers needed to take it easy. Coach Bertman stayed behind, and when he arrived, he was a little upset with my decision, but it worked out. We ended up taking it to them in the first game and won 13 to 5, but rest assured, A&M was saving their ace starter and ace reliever for the night game (the championship game) just in case they lost the first game against McDonald.

The coaching staff was trying to figure out who we were going to have throw in the regional championship game. At this point, our entire pitching staff's arms' were completely spent, worn out. I remember telling Coach Bertman, 'Let's just unscrew a light bulb and have our pitchers throw it against the wall, and the one who is able break it, let's go with him 'cause his arm's the strongest.'

We decided to go with a freshman, Paul Bryd, who really wanted the ball, and he went out there for us and started our last push. Leskanik and McDonald came in at the end to shut them down, and after winning the game 5 to 4, you could see the transformation start. Right there is the point where the LSU baseball program really took off. We were forced to beat somebody tough on the road, and in my opinion, this series catapulted the LSU tradition to where we are today, a program that overcomes difficult odds all because we went to Omaha to the College World Series that year.

Josh Byrnes
[General Manager, Arizona Diamondbacks]
Former Assistant General Manager of the Boston Red Sox

I think baseball is a great, great game. Sometimes it gets criticized, but I think one of the reasons that it does get criticized is because it is held to such a high standard, because people expect so much, which is good. Look at the television ratings. Look at the fact that over 40 million fans are going to Minor League games now. I think the internet has spiked the interest in baseball even more. The interest in numbers and additional availability of stats for comparison from one generation to the next has also had an impact.

There are so many things to gravitate towards within a game, within the season that will follow the off-season. There are a lot of measurable results, a lot of statistics, a lot of pitches, a lot of definable events that feed a lot of people's interests. In fact, the numbers in this game are sacred. Whether it is hitting 30 home runs in a season, hitting 500 for a career, or whether it is getting past home run number 755. These are important barometers in the game. People can look back at Mantle, Mays and Aaron, the guys who set a standard, and go through all the numbers to compare all of the generations of players that followed them.

I have always been passionate about baseball, and I have a lot of vivid memories from the 70's and 80's. As I got older and played in college, I started to understand the business of baseball. As a kid, I wanted to play professionally, but realistically, I knew it was best for me to get into journalism. I started my professional career working with the Cleveland Indians in 1993. This job, the one I have now working in the front office, I guess you could say, fuels my fire. I really love coming into work, knowing there is a win or a loss at the end of the day. Looking back, for me it's obvious why I chose to work with the Boston Red Sox. I felt like the ultimate challenge or the ultimate prize was to be part of a team that wins a World Series with the Red Sox. My dad grew up a big Red Sox fan in New England, and the first World Series that I remember well was the 1975 World Series.

I remember the 2004 World Series, obviously, but it is a little bit of a blur. There was just so much emotion being down three games to none and then to come back against the Yankees. You could argue that we might not have been able to come back against any other team, but because it was the Yankees, the energy we got from our fans in Game 4 of the ALCS, especially when Bill Mueller got the single and Dave Roberts was rounding third to tie the game, put us over the top. Just the reaction of the fans in the stands. These were not the fans who always lost hope, not the so-called "negative Boston fans." They were like, 'We're going to do this!' The Red Sox fan base is tremendous. One of the more vivid memories I have was when we came back to Boston early in the morning from St. Louis after winning the World Series, the spontaneous reactions of people as we traveled back through the city. They were holding up the newspaper and jumping up and down, still cheering—it was incredible.

I felt a lot of satisfaction and a lot of reality on that trip home. Even now, when I think back to the importance of Dave Roberts' stolen base, our season could have ended right there, and that is a fact, the reality of how delicate a balance there is and how many people contributed to give us a chance to win 109 games throughout the course of the regular and post seasons. We just really enjoyed the journey. It was like we knew the script as it was unfolding, and we knew if we could pull this off, it would be one of the great sports stories of all time. Sometimes, you can lose your perspective with the immediacy of the challenge, but we didn't lose it. To our benefit, we continued to go at the game with the mindset, 'Let's see if we can pull this off.'

When we were down three games to none, the city of Boston was down too, but they still believed we could come back. The criticism came at us, rather than praise for the Yankees, but more from the media than from the fans. We were even called a fraud after we had won a 101 games that season. We had been the best team in the game since August 1st. That was a motivating factor when it was time to get to business before Game 4 in the ALCS. Knowing that we couldn't afford another loss, we were really focused on mapping out how to use our pitching to try to get us all the wins we needed. I think Terry Francona, the manager, deserves a ton of credit. He sort of fed off that emotion, and a few players said, 'Don't let us just win one game, because we might just run off four in a row!' It's the way those guys were. They were 8 and 1 in the nine game stretch run in late August and September where everyone was hot. We swept Anaheim, beat Texas two out of three, and swept Oakland. Those guys performed exceptionally well under pressure, and so no one hung their head when we were down three-games to none.

The Yankees are a tough organization to beat. At that time, under Joe Torre, the Yankees had won 17 of 21 playoff series (.809). The Yankees had created a model that was very hard to beat in October, and we felt that they had played exceptionally well in the first three games and we hadn't. As great as Mariano Rivera is, we've beaten him before. That breeds a little bit of confidence, even though we understood that he is one of the best pitchers in baseball. Millar is one of the few players out there who can say he hit a homerun off of Mariano Rivera. That is one of the benefits of familiarity.

Every game had its own story and its own set of questions. We were unsure of Curt Shilling's health in Game 6. Were we using Keith Foulke too much? Where could we get Pedro Martinez in there? Who were we going to have to start Game 7? At the time, Derek Lowe was going to go on only two days rest. Everyone talks about three days rest, but he pitched on two days rest. Some guys were going out there on fumes and just found a way to get it done. I think we were pretty strong in every game, emotionally speaking. Once we got to Game 7, we felt we had a tremendous amount of momentum, and in a lot of ways, we had a lot less to lose than they did. We went out and played a great game, scored early — as we did in a lot of post season games—and Derek Lowe was fantastic. It was just an amazing run. That was sort of the height of it all, but these guys had performed so well in key games the past few years that we were not as surprised as some people might think. We didn't know if we would win, but we knew we would play well. It meant so much to the entire New England area when we won, and I think Jason Varitek put it best when he said, "The fans weren't just saying congratulations, they were saying, *Thank You.*"

Jack McKeon
[Special Advisor, Florida Marlins]

*M*cKeon was originally signed by the Pittsburgh Pirates organization *as a catcher in 1949. In 1951, while serving his country as a member of the armed forces, the then twenty-one year old player/manager led his Sampson (NY) Air Force Base team to the Air Force Championship. After seventeen seasons as a Minor League manager, four-time Manager of the Year (1958 with Missoula, 1961 with Wilson, and 1969 and 1970 with Omaha), McKeon finally got his chance to manage in the Major Leagues and led the Kansas City Royals to second place finish in the AL West division in 1973 with a 88 and 74 record. He later served as the Vice President of Baseball Operations with the San Diego Padres and led them to a World Series against the Detroit Tigers in 1984. On May 11, 2003 McKeon was named Manager of the Florida Marlins and posted a 75-49 record, leading the Marlins to their second World Championship. For the second time in his career (the first time was in 1999 with the Cincinnati Reds), he was named the 2003 National League Manager of the Year by the BBWAA. Jack McKeon "retired" at the end of the 2005 season with the Florida Marlins all-time winning record—241 wins.*

Well, I have a couple of memorable moments that stand out for me. One memorable moment is the first game that I managed in 1973, when I was with the Kansas City Royals. Managing the Royals certainly was the culmination of a lot of years in the bush leagues working my way up, and that job was the achievement of the goal that I had set of reaching the Major Leagues.

The second memorable moment for me was when I was the general manager of the San Diego Padres in 1984 and put together the ball club that went on to win the National League Pennant and went to the World Series.

The 2003 season was pretty memorable too. I was manager of the Florida Marlins and we won the World Championship against the New York Yankees at Yankee Stadium, and being a native of New Jersey and growing up close to Yankee Stadium and visiting the stadium many a time, I had that dream of someday being in the World Series in that great venue. So to get to the Series and for it to be at Yankee Stadium was a dream come true and fantastic.

Chapter 4

The Scribes and Voices

George Will
[Author]

A Pulitzer Prize winning and national best-selling author, George Will is highly regarded as one of the most influential media personalities of his generation. He appeared as a commentator on World News Tonight with Peter Jennings and was a regular member of ABC's This Week on Sunday mornings. The former Michigan State University and University of Toronto professor was educated at Trinity College, Oxford and Princeton Universities. In addition to serving as a staff member for United States Senator Gordon Allot, Will has written several books on the game he truly loves, baseball.

Like a lot of others, I think the most memorable event is the first Major League game that I saw in 1950 at Forbes Field in Pittsburgh. I was with my father, and we were visiting my grandfather, who was a Lutheran Minister in Donora, Pennsylvania, which is famous for being the birthplace of Stan Musial and Ken Griffey Jr. Wally Westlake hit a grand slam home run and beat the Cardinals nine to nothing, and the hit song of the day was "Goodnight Irene" playing all around outside the ballpark.

Jerry Coleman
[Hall of Fame broadcaster, San Diego Padres]

M*r. Jerry Coleman played on six World Series clubs in nine seasons with the New York Yankees. He was an integral part of those teams and helped anchor an infield for arguably one of the greatest sports dynasties of all time. In 1949, Coleman went on to win the Associated Press Rookie of the Year award after hitting .275, driving in 42 runs, and swiping eight bases in his first big league campaign. The following year, he was voted to represent the American League in the All-Star game, and he continued to build on his success by winning the World Series Most Valuable Player honor. Mr. Coleman is also a war hero, serving the United States as a pilot for the Marines in World War II and the Korean War, flying 120 missions and receiving two Distinguished Flying Crosses, thirteen Air Medals, and three Navy Citations. He spent twenty-two years calling games for CBS Radio's Game of the Week and has been the voice of the San Diego Padres for over thirty-two years.*

The most memorable experience for me, and one of the biggest thrills in my life, came in the final game of the 1949 baseball season when we (the New York Yankees) were playing the Boston Red Sox for the pennant. Boston came in to New York with a one game lead and whoever won the two game series went on to the World Series. *The first game of the pivotal two game set happened to be Joe DiMaggio Day at the big ballpark in the Bronx. With the on-field celebration for "Joe D" and the American League pennant on the line, over 69,000 fans crammed themselves into Yankee Stadium to witness one the most anticipated and exhilarating two game series in the history of the American League. The Yankees tied the Red Sox overall win total record by winning the first game of the two game set.*

We beat them 5 to 4 the day before, and it came down to the final game for the pennant. The Red Sox had a better ball club, but we had better pitching and better defense. *In the final game of the regular season, and with the New York Yankees up two runs to zip in the eighth inning, Coleman came up to bat with two outs and the bases loaded. Red Sox pitcher Tex Hughson let a fastball rip that proceeded to move high and tight on the right-handed hitting Coleman. When he swung, he didn't get all of it, but what he did get was enough to be the difference in the ballgame. Coleman's shot fell in between the hard charging right fielder Al Zarilla and second baseman Bobby Doerr. Three runs came in to score to make the score 5 to 0 in the eighth inning.* We ended up beating them 5 to 3, winning the pennant on the final day, and in my mind that is the greatest experience I have had in baseball. To top it all off, it was my rookie year and I thought the world was wonderful.

Dave Campbell
[ESPN Broadcaster]

D ave Campbell is a Major League Baseball analyst for ESPN and formerly worked as a play-by-play commentator and analyst for the Colorado Rockies and San Diego Padres. He played eight seasons in the Major Leagues as an infielder for the Detroit Tigers, San Diego Padres, St. Louis Cardinals, and Houston Astros. While attending the University of Michigan, Campbell was an integral part of their 1962 NCAA National Championship season.

As a player, I think my favorite memory would have to be coming to the big leagues with the team that I grew up with, the Detroit Tigers, and getting my first hit. My first hit was off a guy named Mike Paul, who is a scout to this day, and every time I see him in the pressroom, he goes, 'Oh no, now I got to hear about this...' It was a home run (I was 0 for 7 at the time), and that assuredly stands out.

Being a part-time member of the 1968 World Champion Detroit Tigers stands out as well, although I wasn't on their World Series roster.

As a broadcaster, I would say calling the game in Cincinnati when Pete Rose broke the all-time hit record. I was broadcasting for San Diego at the time. Getting a chance to broadcast the 2002 World Series between the New York Mets and the New York Yankees was also a very memorable experience, but *all* of these baseball memories are great moments for me.

Charley Steiner
[Broadcaster, Los Angeles Dodgers]

*I*n 2002, Steiner joined the New York Yankees radio broadcasts along side John Sterling. In the 2004 season, he started working alongside Vin Scully in the Los Angeles Dodgers radio booth. Prior to working with the Yankees, he was a staple and one of the most beloved anchors on ESPN's SportsCenter.

For me as a broadcaster, the one moment to this point that I always remember is calling Aaron Boone's home run in the bottom half of the 11th inning in Game 7 of the American League Championship Series in 2003. It was a culmination of an extraordinary season, and of an even more amazing American League Championship Series, which was the closest thing to war without gunplay—and the two teams had played each other twenty-six times over the course of a season (the most ever between any two teams). Amazingly, the incredible rivalry between these two clubs and the difference in the season was settled by one pitch and one swing at a quarter past midnight on a Friday morning in October. I guess that is probably the one moment up to this point I will always remember.

Paul Sullivan
[Sportswriter, Chicago Tribune]

I would have to say as a whole, the Sosa–McGwire home run race in 1998 is my favorite baseball memory. It was a little crazy because everyday was something new, and Sammy was just starting to be Sammy then. He was becoming known around the country and just a lot of fun. We also had the pennant race and the Wild Card at the time, and they were all jockeying for position. I think for me that was the most enjoyable time I had covering a season. I have covered baseball since 1989, so I did the '89 Playoffs even though I was the backup guy then. It was still a lot of fun, especially with (Don) Zimmer.

In '84, I covered the Cubs and I worked Metro, but I covered them in the playoffs. There was a tree right outside of Wrigley where people would sit among the branches to view the game, and I climbed it so I could interview people during Game 2 of the National League Championship Series. While I was climbing the tree, my press pass fell off of me. I couldn't climb down to retrieve it, so this guy picks it for me and says, "Don't worry, I'll hold it for you." So I kept climbing and interviewing people who were in the tree watching the game, and when I climbed down the guy had run off with my press pass. I had to talk my way back into the ballpark, and I thought, 'Oh great, my press pass is supposed to last me the entire postseason, through the playoffs *and* the World Series. Now I'm screwed.' As it turned out, they didn't go to the World Series, and in fact, that was their last playoff game there that year.

Gary Miller
[ESPN Broadcaster]

*G*ary *Miller received his Bachelors Degree in radio and television broadcasting from Southern Illinois University in 1978. He worked at CNN as a sports anchor and reporter from 1982 through 1990. Gary joined ESPN in 1990 and has hosted* Baseball Tonight *and been an anchor for* SportsCenter. *Visiting several stadiums while working on this book, I met Gary on several occasions, and his tireless enthusiasm for baseball is virtually unmatched.*

Well, I grew up in Chicago, so my most memorable moment is obviously a heartbreaking one. I don't know if you can count this as a particular moment, but it was the summer of '69, and I remember the local Jewel food stores were having a promotion with coffee mugs with the different infielders' and bullpen pitchers' names etched on them and I had the whole set. I also had all their pictures and watched every game, and as a Cubs fan, watching them collapse in August and September was the most galvanizing thing imaginable, something I have carried all my life. If I had a slogan, it would be Bill Murray's when he filled in for Harry Caray, doing a game against the Expos. His comment had nothing to do with that particular game, but I will always remember that he said, "I hate the Mets worse than communism." That is more than hating the Mets, more than hating the Padres, more than hating all their rivals —and it is more than just loving the Cubs. It is being obsessively in love with the Cubs.

Tom Shaer
[ESPN Radio]

I have had many memorable experiences involving the game of baseball, and one of them will always stand out ahead of the others. This took place recently when I was able to take my (then) seventeen year-old son back to Boston for Games 1 and 2 of the World Series against the St. Louis Cardinals. Just to know that I was getting to share that experience with my son at Fenway Park, and being able to pass that on to him, since I grew up a Red Sox fan, was a great feeling. Being back there to watch the World Series with the Red Sox playing the Cardinals was pretty shocking in the sense that I didn't think they would be in that position in the first place —they were down three games to none to the Yankees in the American League Championship Series. It was almost a miracle! I kept thinking to myself, 'What in the world are we (the Red Sox) doing here, let alone winning the first two games in the World Series?' When Manny Ramirez made those two errors in left field and gave the lead back to the Cardinals, I thought this was going to be another disaster and they would find another way to lose a World Series.

Part of me still cannot believe the Red Sox won it yet. Even though that memory stands out and will forever be cherished, there is still one memory that has never left me, and that was the first Major League game that I saw in person in the summer of 1969.

I grew up in Springfield, Massachusetts, which is about an hour and forty-five minutes away from Fenway Park. Being that far away, we didn't just hop in the car and make a quick drive to see the Sox. I became a Red Sox fan back in 1967, when I was eight years old, because of the "Impossible Dream" American League Pennant-winning Red Sox. Of course, back then, the Red Sox only televised about sixty-five games, and not all of those were covered by the little affiliate station in Springfield, Mass. We would probably only get about forty games a year on TV, and the late box scores from the west coast games were not in the local newspaper. Obviously, there was no internet to log onto to find out what happened either. It was totally different back then. We piled into the car, *we* meaning my two aunts — Aunt Gin and Aunt Mary — their friend, my older brother and myself, and made our way to Fenway Park in the summer of 1969 (July 8th) to see my first game.

We had to wait until the Sox were playing the Detroit Tigers because my aunts' friend who was driving was a Tiger fan. Neither of my aunts drove, and if their friend was going to have to drive all the way to Boston, she at least wanted to wait until she could see the Tigers.

As a kid, you don't really have a concept of how many miles it is from one place to another, or if it's an hour and forty five minutes away... I just remember driving and driving and driving, and thinking, 'Are we *ever* going to get there?' Finally, I saw some buildings out the window that looked like the ones that I had seen as the background in the photos with the players in the team yearbook each year. The Red Sox took the players to various parts of the city to have their picture taken near prominent buildings that would serve as the backdrop. I remembered there was a pitcher named Ken Brett (George Brett's older brother) who had his photo taken in front of the Sears building. Then, before I knew it, there it was, plain as day, the Sears building. I looked over to my right, and there were the light towers on Fenway off in the near distance. Sure enough, we had arrived!

I'll never forget the buzz around the ballpark or the street vendors selling the special afternoon edition of the old Record

American newspapers with a scorecard wrapped around the outside of it for the Red Sox home games. You enter Fenway at ground level, but the field is below street level, so you have to walk up a concrete runway, and for a kid who never had color TV and had never seen the ballpark in color—maybe a few color pictures in the Red Sox yearbook and that's it—that was the biggest of big deals. I vividly remember the green vibrancy of the left field wall known as The Green Monster and the green surface of the field. As a matter of fact, to this day, whenever I go to Fenway Park, I always make sure to come up the same ramp, up the first-base side, and it brings me out to an amazing view of the "Monsta." And that is one of the other things that I remember from that first trip to Fenway: the thick accent of Bostonians, which is much different from the accent in Springfield, Massachusetts. Even though Boston is only an hour and a half away, it might as well be a thousand miles away.

Once you have entered that place, the sounds and smells never leave you. It is a scent of damp concrete and salty popcorn. I still remember seeing the steam rise off of the hot dogs as they were being cooked. All of the sights and sounds of Fenway Park are similar to that of Wrigley Field, but they are distinctly different too. At Fenway, it almost feels like your watching a game in somebody's house. All of the sounds seem to stay in the ballpark, and so what you get at Fenway is a buzz, a constant murmur. The decibel level can go from murmur to buzz to a deafening roar depending on what just happened, but that distinct buzz and murmur are constant. It is always with you when you are at Fenway.

My older brother disappeared in the forth inning to go get popcorn, and back then you could allow an eight-year-old to go and get some popcorn. In the sixth inning, he still hadn't returned, so my aunt sent me to get him. The lines were long and disorganized, and the people kept elbowing their way in front of him, and this poor kid was standing there for two innings with fifty cents trying to get up to the counter and get some popcorn. So I had to show him how to elbow his way in.

Fenway Park has stayed with me my entire life, and been a place where so many memories were made. One of the other memories I hold close to me took place at Fenway too. The last time I saw my dad, before he got sick and subsequently died, was at Fenway in July of 1978. It was the first game after the All-Star break, and we had a nice visit talking and watching the Red Sox together. To this day, when I am back at Fenway and I see Section 29 Row 4 of the grandstand there at Fenway, I remember my dad sitting in the middle of that row to watch his last Red Sox game. Whenever I am there, he is still there with me.

Chapter 5

From Out of the Cornfield

If you have ever had the chance to spend an afternoon at the Field of Dreams in Dyersville, Iowa, you know what I mean when I say there is no other baseball diamond in the world quite like this one. It doesn't have the gargantuan surrounding walls with enormous light towers like old Tiger Stadium in Detroit or Yankee Stadium in New York, but even as you drive up the dusty driveway, you know it's a special ballpark. This is a ballpark that feels as if it has been dropped right out of the sky and into a lush cornfield with a beautiful countryesque white house and old burnt-red barn. After seeing the movie a few hundred times and then finally getting the chance to see the ball field with own my eyes, I have to admit that I was rendered speechless — and as those dearest to me can attest, that in itself can be quite a difficult feat.

I pulled up the worn loose dirt driveway and immediately felt chills travel up and down my spine. The field along the left side of the Lansing's house was just as I had imagined it would be, perhaps a little more worn than fifteen years earlier but still wonderfully vibrant. The field and encompassing lawn still looked to be in top shape. Little did I know that, thanks to Becky Lansing and her tractor mower, this place remains game-ready any day of the week.

I made the relatively easy three and a half hour drive from the Chicagoland suburbs and through the Iowa cornfields in virtually a flash. Upon my arrival, I found myself sitting in the gravel parking area and glancing into my rearview mirror. I could see the giant row of pine trees lined up between the right field line and the fabled house. They towered over the cornfield and appeared to be watching over this sacred land much like the guards at Buckingham Palace protect that edifice and its inhabitants. The Field of Dreams is quite honestly that type of sacred land, a place where you find yourself believing that Shoeless Joe and a group of other ballplayers really came back to play a wonderful game. I don't know if I felt Shoeless Joe's spirit come alive there as I sat in the wooden bleachers and gazed out over the field, but there was no doubt that my spirit sure did.

I met a family with four children who had driven from the west coast to play together on this field for one afternoon. The parents loved the movie and wanted to share the special bond between fiction and reality with their children that this place represents. There was also an older husband and wife who had spent the afternoon taking in the scenery and enjoying the sun-filled sky. Periodically, they would stand up from their big plaid blanket draped over the grass on the third base side of the field, where you might find a bullpen in a Minor League stadium, and casually walk around the perimeter of the field, hand in hand, intermittently talking to one another, perhaps rekindling a friendship and a marriage. There were fathers and sons there as well, an uncle with his niece and nephew, and a group of brothers all carrying their gloves, filling their minds with memories and fulfilled dreams.

One of the special things about baseball is that every person can have their own field of dreams in their own backyard. It can be in a driveway with a taped strike zone on the garage. It can be between buildings in an apartment complex. It can be the local park district field. Your field of dreams can be anywhere you want it to be, because when you are out there at shortstop or in the outfield and you catch a line drive that (in your mind) you are sure no one else could have gotten to, in that brief moment, you are immortal. You can fulfill your dreams everyday—baseball permits this, it encourages it.

Watching the games on television is great, but I suggest you treat yourself to an evening with just the radio and the ballgame. The game becomes more vivid. The colors are more vibrant, because they are in your mind, and you get to decide exactly how the pitcher releases ball and how hard the hitter swings at the pitch.

You get to see the game from the perspective of your mind's eye while visualizing the account of the game as you listen to the call of the radio announcer. It may take a little more imagination to enjoy a game on the radio, but baseball is a kid's game, and we all have a little kid in us despite our age, and so we come to the task well equipped.

The Field of Dreams is precisely the type of place that you can visit and transform time. You can be a kid again, a father, a mother, a son, a daughter. You can have a game of catch. You can play a nine inning game. You can sit on the bleachers and reminisce. You can bring a picnic basket loaded with sandwiches and soda and spend an afternoon playing at the same ballpark that the great Shoeless Joe walked onto and spoke with Ray Kinsella.

When I spoke to some of the college coaches, Major League ballplayers, and executives whose stories are chronicled in this book, I asked them a very simple question that caused them to think about this place just a little differently than a moment before: "If you could have one person come out the magical cornfield from the movie, *Field of Dreams* to have a catch with, who would it be? I told them it could be anyone: a family member, a former player—anyone with whom they would like to have a game of catch."

Following Jude Milbert's story you'll see their answers. Before you read their answers, however, I would like for you to think for a second and answer that question for yourself.

If it is possible, I strongly encourage you to pick up the phone, send an email, or send a letter to the person that you would like to have a catch with while you still have the chance. And if it isn't possible because the person you have chosen is no longer with us, perhaps an old ballplayer or a loved one, send the request out there with your mind anyway. Who knows, maybe the *Field of Dreams* might grant you one incredible game of catch...

Jude Milbert
[Portrayed a St. Louis Cardinal in "Fields of Dreams"]

It has been great to be a part of something that was nominated for an Academy Award, but more importantly, it has been great to be part of something that has brought a lot of good to so many people. There have been so many remarkable stories about people and how they have been affected by the Field since the movie came out. No matter how many different stories I hear, it always pulls at me. We had no idea that the finished movie would be as big as it was. The number of people who have come out here to Dyersville has been remarkable. Over the years, there have been unbelievable stories written in the local newspaper about sons and fathers meeting out there, either for the first time or rekindling a relationship with each other. Or there are other stories about people who were adopted and came over to the Field to meet their biological parents for the first time.

There have been so many wonderful personal moments at the Field too. On my mother's 80th birthday, shortly after the movie came out, we started a tradition by gathering everyone in our family from across the county every five years to have a birthday party for her and a family reunion at the same time. We always would go to the Field and have a big game with everyone. We always took a bunch of pictures of everyone laughing and having a blast together. Around the time of our first big game there, my mother had taken some pictures of my daughters when they were about four and six. She had taken a shot of one of the girls standing at home plate holding a bat and my other daughter sitting on the bleachers. My mother just passed away recently, and when we were going through her things, we found that she had two large pictures of the girls from that first trip to the Field of Dreams. She had put notes on them, telling us how much she enjoyed going out there and she wanted to make sure the girls got these pictures with all of them having fun together at the Field of Dreams. My girls are in college now, but when we saw those pictures, it immediately brought back a ton of wonderful memories.

The opportunity to be a part of this all started rather inconspicuously for me. There were some articles in the local newspapers saying that a movie production was looking for a bunch of ballplayers who were over 30 years old and who were interested in being in a film. Since semi-pro baseball is still pretty active around here, it wasn't a problem getting players. A group of us from the surrounding area went to one of the local colleges in Dubuque, Iowa for the tryout. When we arrived, there were at least two or three hundred guys already there who were interested in being in the movie too. I guess we didn't realize that they had 'advertised' not only in Iowa but in nearby states as well. We went through the tryouts and proceeded to go through a number of baseball drills. They ended up selecting quite a few players from the immediate area of Dyersville, which worked out great because of a lot of us were already friends.

For over a year prior to the filming of the movie, *Field of Dreams*, the Dyersville Iowa area was in a severe drought and everything in the area seemed brown and lifeless. It seemed to get hotter and hotter each day. Since the baseball field was going to be the centerpiece of the movie, it had to look pristine, and by the time filming was scheduled to begin, it sure did! The production team irrigated the field regularly by pumping water from a nearby stream. The field and the general area around it that became known as "the set" was completely off limits while they prepared it for filming. So when we, the team of movie ballplayers, pulled up the driveway for our first look, I think we all had the same reaction: WOW! We couldn't believe it! Here was this manicured, picture perfect, green field right before us and we couldn't wait to play ball on it!

The late Rod Dedeaux, the former USC baseball and Olympic head coach, and Don Buford were there as consultants for us as we practiced. Don Buford ran the practices and took us through drills. We spent a lot of time working on using the smaller gloves like the old players used for more of an authentic feel. We had to learn how to field with them, how to turn double plays, and field cutoffs now using two hands. We would normally go in for a good two or three-hour practice every day for a week.

One of the things that I remember that really got us going was when they were filming some of the scenes with Frank Dardas, who was Ray Liotta's stand-in for Shoeless Joe, fielding the ball. It is important to let you know that Frank's a good player and a real competitor. One of the guys who was hitting the ball out to him took one deep and it was headed for the corn. Frank was going after it full speed, and at the last second he made a diving catch while knocking down about four or five corn stalks in the cornfield behind the outfield in the process. All of the baseball players who were watching this went crazy because it was such a great catch, but the directors and producers were going crazy because he had taken out a huge patch of the corn. It was funny how the same event caused two completely different reactions!

Kevin Costner was a lot of fun to be around and is such a great guy. He loved to play catch, and he really loved to play pepper. There is a lot of downtime on a movie set, and one of the great things he did to make it more enjoyable was always starting up games of pepper. We played pepper all the time. He would bat, and the last person standing would win dinner, on him. Other times, Timothy Busfield, who loved to play cards, would come over to where we had a card table set up and play cards with us. We taught him a couple of Midwestern card games like Spades and Euchre. It was great sitting around talking baseball. James Earl Jones was very friendly and very approachable too. If we were standing around waiting for the next scene to take place, he would come over and talk with us. The actors and movie staff turned out to be a great group of people. Thinking back, it still feels good to be a part of something special for so many people.

Coco Crisp's *answer to the* Field of Dreams *question:* **Josh Gibson.** Even though he wasn't a Major League player, he was one of the greatest home run hitters of all time, and he could have been one of the greatest home run hitters in the Major Leagues but never got the opportunity. I have watched movies from back in the day, and he seemed like a fun guy to be able to talk to, someone to learn a few things from about how to play.

◆ ◆ ◆

Jody Davis' *answer to the* Field of Dreams *question:* It would have to be a toss up between two guys I didn't get a chance to play against, the first being **Roberto Clemente** and the second being **J.R. Richard** from the Houston Astros. The guys that I played with, we used to talk about some of the great pitchers of the era that we faced like Nolan Ryan, and the guys that I talked to said, 'Man J.R. Richard is the best!' Thank goodness I didn't have to face him, but I sure would have liked to have caught him just to see what it was like.

◆ ◆ ◆

Mark Loretta's *answer to the* Field of Dreams *question:* I have always admired **Jackie Robinson** and been a big fan of his, and I think it would be a great thing to have a catch with him for all the things he's done for the country in general. I think he would be a great guy to have a catch with.

◆ ◆ ◆

Todd Walker's *answer to the* Field of Dreams *question:* My **granddad,** who passed away a few years ago. I would have liked to have seen him when he was young because he was a four sport athlete and very involved in a lot of different things. Back in the day, he was also a pilot. So, if I had to choose one person to have a catch with, it would be **Don Spargo,** my mom's dad. He was an incredible person, and I would have really liked the chance to see him in his prime.

◆ ◆ ◆

Harold Baines' *answer to the* Field of Dreams *question:* My **father.** He is still living and he had the talent, but never had a chance to take it very far. To be able to see him in a Major League uniform would be very special.

◆ ◆ ◆

Eric Munson's *answer to the* Field of Dreams *question:* **Ted Williams.** He was the greatest hitter to ever live. My dad grew up in Vermont where everyone is a big Red Sox fan, and after watching his tapes and seeing Williams hit and hearing some of his interviews, I think meeting him would be pretty cool.

◆ ◆ ◆

Jorge Posada's *answer to the* Field of Dreams *question:* Both of my **grandparents.** They were huge baseball fans, and they never got to see me play in the big leagues. I would love to have at least one day where they could see me play a little ball.

◆ ◆ ◆

John Olerud's *answer to the* Field of Dreams *question:* I would have to say **Rogers Hornsby.** The major reason I say that is, not only was he a great player, but the scout that signed my dad had a good relationship with Mr. Hornsby and at Christmas time when we would get together with him he would tell us all of these Rogers Hornsby stories. Again not only was he a great player, but he is also somebody I have heard a bunch of interesting stories about and I think it would be fun to play catch with him.

Mark Prior's *answer to the* Field of Dreams *question:* I'd have to go with either **Babe Ruth** or **Ty Cobb**. Those were a couple of the original guys that really symbolized the game. It doesn't matter if their records are broken or not broken — they'll always be remembered for what they contributed to the game.

♦♦♦

Phil Nevin's *answer to the* Field of Dreams *question:* My **dad**. Obviously, it would be a special moment for both of us, but more importantly, what it would mean to him would give me a great feeling. We never get a chance to do that anymore. When I was a kid we played catch, but after I went to high school and college, he became a big fan and just watched instead of participated. For him to be able to participate now and create something like that would be pretty special.

♦♦♦

Charley Steiner's *answer to the* Field of Dreams *question:* **Babe Ruth** was not only the greatest baseball player of all time. He was a larger than life personality. Here it is now (almost 80) years after he hit his 60th homerun and he is still regarded as the quintessential baseball player. All you have to do is say the Babe and everyone knows who he is and I hope it would be a good long catch because we have a whole heck of a lot to talk about.

♦♦♦

Tim Hudson's *answer to the* Field of Dreams *question:* **Abner Doubleday** – to be able to have a catch with him and ask him why in the world he invented this game?

Frank McCourt's *answer to the* Field of Dreams *question:* No question, it's my **dad.** He brought me to my first game and passed on his love of the game. I think about him every day, and I think it would be unbelievable to see him come out of the cornfield and we could see one another and have a catch—that would be great.

◆ ◆ ◆

Dontrelle Willis' *answer to the* Field of Dreams *question:* **Shoeless Joe.** I would just ask him to tell me about his road and hear his stories and hear about everything they went through.

◆ ◆ ◆

Tony Muser's *answer to the* Field of Dreams *question:* My **dad.** I lost him when I was twenty-two and he was only forty-nine years old. It would be a great thrill to have the chance to play catch with him. On the professional side, if I could have a catch with anyone who played big league ball, I would say **Stan Musial.** Musial had a very unusual stance and a great swing and was somebody I grew up admiring. I think if I could play catch with Stan Musial that would be something.

◆ ◆ ◆

Rich Aurilia's *answer to the* Field of Dreams *question:* My **high school coach.** He meant more to me than just a high school coach, and for the past ten years I have not been able to see him a lot. So, to sit down and talk a little bit would be great.

◆ ◆ ◆

Jason Varitek's *answer to the* Field of Dreams *question:* I think it would have to be both of my **grandfathers.** My mom's dad didn't get to see me play much, and my dad's dad got to see me play only a little bit, and both would really enjoy the fact that we could all play catch.

190

Ellis Burks' *answer to the* Field of Dreams *question:* I would have to say **Josh Gibson** is who I'd like to play catch with. He never made it to the Major Leagues, but he had the talent. At that time, there were only one or two African-Americans in the big leagues, guys like Jackie Robinson and Satchel Paige, so it was more of a numbers game. But Gibson had the stats to just die for. If you look back in the Negro League archives and find his numbers, you'll see that they were phenomenal!

♦ ♦ ♦

Juan Pierre's *answer to the* Field of Dreams *question:* I would like to have a game of catch with **Darryl Strawberry.** I loved him growing up. In my parent's house, I still have Darryl Strawberry posters up on the walls everywhere. I didn't pattern myself after him game-wise because he was more of a power guy and I am more of a speed guy, but he was just one of those guys that I always followed and had all of his baseball cards and hats and everything. He is one guy I would love to play catch with and sit down and talk to.

♦ ♦ ♦

Paul Konerko's *answer to the* Field of Dreams *question:* **Babe Ruth.** I mean who wouldn't want to have a catch with Babe Ruth?

♦ ♦ ♦

Mark Mulder's *answer to the* Field of Dreams *question:* **Shoeless Joe Jackson.** I would love to talk to him and find out about the whole scandal — what really happened. Growing up in Chicago, you hear about it a lot, and it would be great to find out exactly what took place.

John Schuerholz's *answer to the* Field of Dreams *question:* There are a lot great players that I have been fortunate to associate with and to have seen play in my 40 years of being involved in the game, and even before that, while growing up and just loving the game as a fan, but I would have to say my **dad.** He was the one who introduced me to the game. He played professional baseball for three years in the Minor Leagues, and he really started my interest in the game and helped foster my love for the game. He taught me so many things about this game that I would not know even where to begin the list.

♦ ♦ ♦

George Horton's *answer to the* Field of Dreams *question:* I would say **Babe Ruth** would be my choice for a game of catch. I would like to ask Babe a few questions about on and off the field stuff. Not only was he one of the best baseball players of all time, but he had the most impact on our industry in the things he did off the field for people, the statement that he made. He is probably the most intriguing guy who has ever achieved great success in the game, and I would love to have a catch with him.

♦ ♦ ♦

Tony Peña's *answer to the* Field of Dreams *question:* I would have to say that my choice would be between my **wife** and my **mom.** My mom was the one who introduced me to the game, and she was the one who pitched to me the first time, and my wife has been with me so long throughout my career. But as far as a player goes, I would definitely choose **Johnny Bench** to play a little catch with and get some of his insights into the game.

♦ ♦ ♦

George Will's *answer to the* Field of Dreams *question:* **Jackie Robinson.**

♦ ♦ ♦

Khalil Greene's *answer to the* Field of Dreams *question:* Growing up, I was a Pirates fan because I was born in Pittsburgh and both my parents were born and raised in Pittsburgh. So I would say **Roberto Clemente.** I never got to see him play other than highlights or video clips, so I think to be able to see him play in person would be pretty neat.

♦ ♦ ♦

Lance Parrish's *answer to the* Field of Dreams *question:* **Ty Cobb,** because I was signed by the Detroit Tigers out of high school and I have played the better part of my career with the Tigers. Ty Cobb has such a huge legacy, not only in the game of baseball, but here with the Detroit Tigers, and I think it would be interesting to meet him since he was such a colorful character as well. A lot of people have different opinions of him, and I wouldn't mind playing catch with him and then sitting down and just talking for awhile.

♦ ♦ ♦

Chris Chambliss' *answer to the* Field of Dreams *question:* My **grandfather.** I knew the man, but I didn't get to know like I really would have liked to, and getting the chance to talk with him again would be unbelievable.

♦ ♦ ♦

Josh Beckett's *answer to the* Field of Dreams *question:* **Nolan Ryan** would be my choice. Even though I know him, I think to be able to play catch with him would be fun!

♦ ♦ ♦

Mike Gillespie's *answer to the* Field of Dreams *question:* I think that **Jackie Robinson** would be my choice for a game of catch. It just seems foreign to us today that there was a time that Negro League players, black players, were not allowed to play Major League Baseball. Jackie Robinson, without doubt, changed baseball forever, but he really changed U. S. history. Unfortunately, segregation was alive and well in 1947 when he first played in the Major Leagues. I think the fact that he played in the big leagues made a significant difference in our society, let alone what it has done for baseball. Now we are able to see not only a number of black players, but an increasing number of Latin players and international players, including more and more Asian players. Jackie Robinson was the beginning of the evolution of the game to an international sport. None of us can really relate to what Jackie Robinson experienced back then as he went from place to place to play baseball, and so we can't understand how tough he had to be. That would be the guy that I would have a catch with, even though he was a Bruin.

Steve Finley's *answer to the* Field of Dreams *question:* I would like to play catch with **Lou Gehrig.** Cal Ripken taught me a lot about the game and how to play it, and I think that Cal had a lot of the same traits that Lou Gehrig had — going out there every single day and playing hard and playing it right. I would just like to be around him, play catch with him, and talk to him about how he went about his business. I like trying to play the game right and learning from guys who did it the best — and Lou Gehrig certainly did it right.

Kelly McCord's *answer to the* Field of Dreams *question*: That person would be my **great-grandmother,** Ruby McCord. She was such an amazing and strong woman, and she taught me not to give up and to follow my dreams. I think she would be so proud to know that, after nine years of battling and trying to prove myself, all of the hard work finally paid off. She lived to be 96 years old, and she believed that, with hard work and passion for what you believe in, you can achieve your dreams.

Kenny Lofton's *answer to the* Field of Dreams *question*: **Satchel Paige**. He was a well-known pitcher back in the Negro Leagues, and he was a guy on top of his game. He was finally, even though at an older age, able to play in the big leagues. I mean, for him to endure what he had to in order to be able to pitch in the big leagues is inspiring. Just his style was something I would want to see, and I would love the chance to play catch with him.

Mike Lowell's *answer to the* Field of Dreams *question*: **Roberto Clemente** would be my choice, because when my dad left Cuba for Puerto Rico, he would always say that Clemente was not only one of the greatest players but one of the nicest guys he had ever known. My dad gave me a painting of Roberto Clemente that I still have. I have always put him on a pedestal. I obviously never got a chance to see him play, so that would be pretty awesome to have a catch with the great Roberto Clemente — and it would be pretty fun for me!

Barry Larkin's *answer to the* Field of Dreams *question*: I would like to have a game of catch with **Jackie Robinson,** because he was a trailblazer and I would like to talk to him about some of the things he had to endure. He is one of the reasons that I am here today. He opened a lot of doors, and his sacrifices gave a lot of us the opportunity to play. People like that don't get the appreciation they deserve.

◆◆◆

David McCarty's *answer to the* Field of Dreams *question*: One person I would like to play catch with would be my **grandfather.** He died in 1985, and I would love a chance to play catch and talk with him again.

◆◆◆

Tony LaRussa's *answer to the* Field of Dreams *question*: **Bill Veeck**

◆◆◆

Paul Mainieri's *answer to the* Field of Dreams *question*: If I could have one person come out of the cornfield to play catch with on my field of dreams, it would be **Lou Gehrig.** When I was a young child growing up in the 60's (I was born in '57), we didn't have a lot of different television stations like there are now. Basically, there were three major network stations. It seemed that the movie *Pride of the Yankees* was on at least once a year on one of those stations. I must have watched that movie, with Gary Cooper playing Lou Gehrig, ten times over a few years. I just grew up admiring him so much for so many reasons – his humility even though he was one of the greatest players of his time, his toughness, his work ethic and how he played every day for so many years, his dedication to the team, how he loved his parents so much, how he was dedicated to a wonderful wife, and then, finally, how he showed such great courage in the face of a terrible disease. I cried every time I watched that movie because of the way it ended with his death, but it taught me at a young age to never take anything for granted. Next to the *Pride of the Yankees, Field of Dreams* is my favorite movie. What a great movie because it demonstrated the purity and beauty of the game, as well as the infatuation with the sport that so many feel. In the end, the great thing about the movie was not so much the baseball theme of the movie, however, but that, through baseball, it was made possible to undo any regrets that one might have in life, to go back and change things in your life because baseball opens the door – what a great dream!

Josh Byrnes' *answer to the* Field of Dreams *question*: **Jackie Robinson.** I think he did more for this game than anyone else, and in a lot of ways, he did much for society as a whole. His accomplishment is even apparent today in how people conduct themselves, whether it is in a sport or elsewhere. His personal code, his integrity, and what he had to deal with made him a special ballplayer. I don't think anyone could have personified grace under pressure as well as he did.

♦ ♦ ♦

Jack McKeon's *answer to the* Field of Dreams *question*: My **father** would be my choice for a game of catch. He was a hard working guy who died at the age of 59. He was really dedicated to making life easier for his wife and his four children, and to that end he went overboard. I mean, he was a workaholic in order to provide all the good things in life for us, and he was the guy who made sure that we had baseball teams, equipment, basketball equipment and facilities to practice in — and I think he more or less molded all the young kids in the area to use sports as a way of succeeding in life and to get away from evil elements. He started a Boys Club during the Second World War, and we had fifteen members. He provided us transportation and support. Out of those fifteen guys, three of them made the Major Leagues. Johnny and Eddie O'Brien and myself. Johnny went on to be an All-American in basketball too.

◆ ◆ ◆

John Smoltz's *answer to the* Field of Dreams *question:* **Shoeless Joe Jackson** would be my choice for a game of catch. I would like to know how bad he did get robbed and what the real scenario was. I can't imagine being banned for something you didn't do or being falsely accused, let alone the ramifications of how it changed his life.

◆ ◆ ◆

Roberto Alomar's *answer to the* Field of Dreams *question:* **Roberto Clemente.** He was a person that helped to open the door for the Latin players and in fact, was one of the greatest players of all time. We came from the same country, but I was too young when he was playing to recognize how great he was. To be able to play catch with him would be awesome.

◆ ◆ ◆

Barry Zito's *answer to the* Field of Dreams *question:* It would definitely be **Sandy Koufax,** because I look up to him as a left-handed pitcher. His curve ball was so dominating, and as a pitcher he was so dominating too, but he was a real icon in the Jewish culture as well. He is a guy I would love to see throw. I have seen a little video on him, but to be able to play catch with him would be cool.

◆ ◆ ◆

Johnny Damon's *answer to the* Field of Dreams *question:* I would have to say **Ronald Regan** because of what he represented and what he stood for. He was the Hollywood movie star and played the Gipper, and of course he was also the Governor of California and the President. Everything about Ronald Regan stated perfection.

♦ ♦ ♦

Dave Campbell's *answer to the* Field of Dreams *question:* I think it would have to be my **dad.** He was a high school baseball coach, and he taught me about 90% of what I learned in the game. I don't think I ever got a chance to thank him before he passed away and I would make sure I did this time.

♦ ♦ ♦

Tim Wallach's *answer to the* Field of Dreams *question:* **Willie Mays.**

♦ ♦ ♦

Dave Roberts' *answer to the* Field of Dreams *question:* Without a doubt it would be **Jackie Robinson.** He meant a lot to the game of baseball, and because I am half African American, I realize that he paved the way for African Americans. Having played for the Dodgers and being a part of the Dodger family for years in my career makes that choice even more special. The opportunity to play catch with Jackie Robinson would be my wish.

♦ ♦ ♦

Jim Edmonds' *answer to the* Field of Dreams *question:* I would probably like to see **Babe Ruth** walk out of that cornfield. I mean, I really appreciate what he did for the game. We looked up his stats one time we were in Chicago, and his offensive and

Steve Sullivan

pitching stats were unbelievable. I think that is very unique, and being a pitcher when I was younger, I always wished I could pitch and play offense with that level of equal skill. I always thought that was unbelievable, and that he was the king of baseball. To see what he did in the game of baseball is pretty impressive.

◆ ◆ ◆

"Smoke" Laval's *answer to the* Field of Dreams *question:* It would have to be **Babe Ruth.** I grew up being a catcher and idolized Johnny Bench, and I got to see him play, got his autograph, but Babe Ruth — he *is* baseball. I know people are going to continue to break the homerun record, like Hank Aaron did and Barry Bonds will do soon, but Ruth brought the game to where it is. When you think of baseball—it's like when you think of peanut butter and jelly or bacon and eggs—it's baseball and Babe Ruth.

I could tell some of these kids that I work with nowadays, 'Wow, you just threw it like Bench,' and a few of these kids wouldn't know who I am referring to, but if you say 'you hit a Ruthian shot,' or 'not even Ruth could have hit the ball that far,' and everyone in baseball knows you mean Babe Ruth. There has never been someone who was like the Babe in any other sport. Michael Jordan was great in basketball, Muhammad Ali was a great boxer, but there will only be one Babe Ruth. So it would be my great honor to have a catch with the Babe. I think I would probably put in a little chew, play some catch, and talk a little baseball with the Babe. Man, would that be something!

◆ ◆ ◆

Kevin Tower's *answer to the* Field of Dreams *question:* I would have to say **Roberto Clemente.** After spending a couple of years in Pittsburgh where Clemente played for his Major League career, being a part of the Pirate organization and hearing the great stories about him, and when you think of how he lost his life heading to Nicaragua at the time to help earthquake victims, I would definitely say Roberto Clemente. He was trying to bring relief to the people there, and unfortunately, his plane crashed off the coast of Puerto Rico. What he meant to baseball and the way he played the game are both remarkable. Major League Baseball named the good guy award in baseball for Roberto Clemente, and he would be the person I would choose to play catch with.

Jeff Pentland's *answer to the* Field of Dreams *question:* My **dad** would be one person I'd choose to play catch with. He taught me the importance of going to work everyday, and he taught me another valuable lesson: don't let anybody influence you unless you want to be influenced by them. He taught me to respect but never fear people. That was the greatest advice he gave me.

Sean Casey's *answer to the* Field of Dreams *question:* Well, I'd choose someone not in the movie, someone who never played pro ball. Both of my **grandmothers.** Unfortunately, my nana, whose dream was to see me playing here in the big leagues, passed away right before I made it. My mom's mom, who passed away a long time ago, even before my mom was married, would be the other. I have heard so many funny stories about her and heard that she was such a great lady. So, to be able to meet her and have all three of us out there and to have three-way game of catch together would be pretty awesome!

Shawn Green's *answer to the* Field of Dreams *question:* I think it would be my **grandfather.** He passed away about ten years ago, but to have a catch with him when he was younger would be great.

◆◆◆

Ozzie Guillen's *answer to the* Field of Dreams *question:* **Roberto Clemente** would be my choice for someone to have a catch with, because he opened the door for a lot of people over here and he was my hero. I never met him, and I always wished that could have happened for me. So Roberto would be the man for me.

◆◆◆

Pokey Reese's *answer to the* Field of Dreams *question:* I would have to say my **great-granddad.** He was a big-time Braves fan, and I would listen to the games with him on the radio when I was little. We didn't have cable TV so we would listen to the games on the radio. He would have loved to see me playing in the big leagues right now."

◆◆◆

Bobby Cox's *answer to the* Field of Dreams *question:* If I could play catch with anybody, it would be **Babe Ruth.** I would love to be able to talk with the Babe. It would be a dream, the ultimate dream to talk to and have a catch with Babe Ruth. I don't think there will ever be another Babe Ruth. He *was* baseball. He was a true character of the game. There were better hitters, but Babe's combination of character and ability was unique. As far as that goes, Babe is going to win every time.

◆◆◆

During the process of completing this first book in the **Talking...Amongst Friends** series, I found that most everyone has a great baseball story from somewhere in their past. If you would like to share your story with us and possibly be in a future edition of Talking Baseball...Amongst Friends, please go to our website, **www.talkingaf.com** to submit your story.

With every *Talking Baseball Amongst Friends* book that is sold, Shamrock Publishing Group will donate a portion of the revenues to The Perfect Game Foundation, a 501 c3 Foundation.